THE ROMANCE OF ELSEWHERE

The Romance
of Elsewhere

ESSAYS

LYNN FREED

COUNTERPOINT

BERKELEY

First Counterpoint hardcover edition: June 2017

Library of Congress Cataloging-in-Publication Data
Names: Freed, Lynn, author.
Title: The romance of elsewhere : essays / Lynn Freed.
Description: Berkeley, CA : Counterpoint, 2017.
Identifiers: LCCN 2017005011 | ISBN 9781619029279 (hardback)
Subjects: | BISAC: LITERARY COLLECTIONS / Essays. | BIOGRAPHY & AUTOBIOGRAPHY / Women. | BIOGRAPHY & AUTOBIOGRAPHY / Personal Memoirs.
Classification: LCC PR9369.3.F68 A6 2017 | DDC 824/.914—dc23
LC record available at https://lccn.loc.gov/2017005011

Paperback ISBN: 978-1-64009-159-7

Cover design by Kelly Winton
Interior design by Domini Dragoone

Counterpoint
2560 Ninth Street, Suite 318
Berkeley, CA 94710
www.counterpointpress.com

Printed in the United States of America

For Georgia

Contents

THE ROMANCE OF ELSEWHERE

The Romance of Elsewhere

FROM A VERY EARLY AGE I HAVE SUFFERED A VERSION OF Baudelaire's *l'horreur du domicile* (horror of the home), an aversion that seems to coexist nicely with a strong attachment to the comfort, the privacy, the intimacy, and the pride of home. I'm not sure how this happened, this pull of the strange against the familiar and back again, but I do know that the rhythm of leaving and returning has kept me nicely unsettled for more than forty-five years. And that without it, I would have drowned any desire to write in restlessness and regret.

Dreams of displacement began for me in childhood. Generally, they centered around something like a steamship, me at the rail, waving at those left behind, or me moving steadily into the distance, with the deck chairs and dancing and dressing for dinner, and time stretching out luxuriously to journey's end. Perhaps the seed for this longing came from my grandmother, who, every year, would take off for England on the Union-Castle, with her trunks and hatboxes, and then go on to America, seeking a cure for her deafness.

Waving her goodbye from the dock, I longed fiercely to be deaf myself, whatever it would take to be the one sailing out of that bay. As I grew older, I would have given much, and still would, to be able to travel as Somerset Maugham did, or Graham Greene, or Lawrence Durrell, or Robert Graves, or D. H. Lawrence—all those Englishmen fleeing their island for somewhere else, somewhere warm, somewhere foreign.

"The moat in Mandalay is one of the minor beauties of the world," wrote Maugham in his notebook. "It has not the sublimity of Kilauea, nor the spectacular picturesque of the Lake of Como, it has not the swooning loveliness of the coastline of a South Pacific island, nor the austere grandeur of parts of the Peloponnesus, but it has a beauty which you can take hold of and enjoy and make your own."

"Were the South Seas really like that?" asked Alec Waugh after reading a few of Maugham's novels. "I had to find out for myself. I bought a round-the-world ticket that included Tahiti . . . I have been on the move ever since."

Before television, before television documentaries, it was largely travel books that opened the door to the world for those left at home. To see that world, and to make money doing so, writers would find themselves a sponsor, then take off for months here, months there, fueled by fierce competition as to who would write first or best about where. One of the chief reasons, for instance, that Rebecca West wrote *Black Lamb and Grey Falcon* was that Yugoslavia had not yet been written up by the competition. With the Nazi threat making itself clear, she had the foresight to grab it before it was overrun, either by Hitler or Stalin.

"IS THERE NO ONE WRITING AT ALL IN ENGLAND NOW?" wrote Lawrence Durrell in 1936, from Corfu. Well, no, most of them were not, certainly not before the Second World War introduced severe restrictions to travel, including passports. Even Evelyn Waugh, who had been rather sour on travel and much else, had been on the hoof for years, writing, among others, six books on travel. One of them, *Labels*, resulted from his literary agent's arranging a free cruise around the Mediterranean for Waugh and his wife (also called Evelyn, or "She-Evelyn," as Waugh referred to her), in return for some praise, duly delivered. (Which puts me in mind of Bulgari paying the British novelist Fay Weldon to mention its product at least a dozen times in one of her novels. And she did. And the novel rather fizzled.)

*

MY FIRST CHANCE to be lifted out of South Africa and into what was fondly considered "the real world" came to me at the age of eighteen in the form of an American Field Service exchange scholarship. Overseas travel then was ruinously expensive for South Africans. Even my parents, who had spent years in England as students, hadn't left South Africa again since their marriage thirty-odd years before. And so, when the chance came for me, however miscast I knew myself to be for the role of emissary, I grabbed it.

If there's any rule that applies to travel, it seems to be that it was so much better a generation or two before. Certainly, I was a few generations too late for the sort of thrilling journey that had Beryl Markham, for instance, making her way up Africa in a single-engine plane, trying to reach Cairo without plunging into the Sudd. By the time I flew to Cairo—and then to Frankfurt, and then to Shannon, and then, at last, to New York—it was in what was then a modern four-engine prop, with about eighty other foreign exchange students, all of us hitting the airport tourist shops along the way. (I still have the small leather camel

I bought at the Cairo airport, far more charming than the real camels I would encounter twenty-odd years later, when I returned to Egypt. There it is, in the back of a cupboard, an *aide-mémoire* for that first long journey out.)

Already, on the plane, I had begun what would become a monstrous accumulation of *aide-mémoire*—letters home to my parents, which, over the year and the years that followed, constituted what amounted to a performance of my life for their audience. At first the letters assumed the voice of a heroic reporter from the front—or, rather, from some uncharted frontier—providing observations and commentary for those unlucky enough to have been left behind. The farther away I got, the more romantic seemed the distance between us. I even envied the students being sent on to California, not because I knew enough about California to want to go there, but because it was farther still than New York, where I was to remain.

If this is madness, I wasn't alone in it. There has always been romance in distance—a shallow romance, certainly. But it has its corollary in the fact that home is so very unromantic. There, among the clatter of knives and forks, the phone going, the laundry piling up, the heart tends to stay still, at least for me. And a still heart doesn't do much for the imagination. Which is not to say there are not wonderful writers who seldom venture far from home—of course there are. One doesn't hear of William Faulkner hopping a freighter to Tahiti, or Robert Frost striking out for Kashmir. Perhaps the delight in placing oneself as a stranger in a strange place is a form of derangement, from which they, and others like them, are and were happily spared.

Whatever the case, there I was, half deranged with delight at the thought of being in New York, half a world away from home. We were staying in dormitories at the AFS headquarters, down near the UN, and as soon as I could escape the endless orientations, I plunged out into the stifling throb and swirl of the city.

At the bottom of Forty-second Street, I joined a crowd climbing onto a bus. "Does this bus go uptown or downtown?" I asked the driver. I'd acquired the terms from a guidebook I'd picked up at AFS headquarters. They meant nothing to me, uptown or downtown or anywhere else, but it was lovely to be able to try them out on a native.

The bus driver banged the palm of his hand violently on the steering wheel. "Shut up," he said, "get on, don't ask questions."

And I couldn't have been more delighted had I been Cortés encountering Montezuma for the first time.

Perhaps it was at that moment that my love affair with New York really began. And it remains for me the only city in the world in which I feel completely at home. I put this down in no small part to the fact that it is full of people as mad as that bus driver, but also because it is a city for the displaced, a virtual celebration of displacement, with little sense, except in certain shops or restaurants or clubs, that one has entered a sort of Whartonesque world, in which one is not qualified for membership. Joining the throng, I still feel marvelously foreign, gloriously myself, wonderfully free.

Henry James, writing of London in 1881, could have been describing just such a New York in the early sixties. "It is not a pleasant place," he wrote. "It is not agreeable, or cheerful, or easy, or exempt from reproach. It is only magnificent. You can draw up a tremendous list of reasons why it should be insupportable. The fogs, the smoke, the dirt, the darkness, the wet, the distance, the ugliness, the brutal size of the place, the horrible numerosity of society, the manner in which this senseless bigness is fatal to amenity, to convenience, to conversation, to good manners . . . dreary, heavy, stupid, dull, inhuman, vulgar at heart and tiresome in form. But . . . [it] is on the whole the most possible form of life."

I should add here that, when I returned to New York from South Africa four years later, married and a graduate student, I didn't feel the least bit free. I felt stuck; I *was* stuck. And I found myself missing grass to walk on and an unimpeded view of the sky. I was sick to death of the perpetual traffic noise, the airbrakes of the trucks shuddering to a halt outside my bedroom window, and of the dirt, and of the madwoman on the bench in the middle of 113th Street, screaming at me daily to wash what I understood, at first, to be my cat.

*

DURING MY EXCHANGE-STUDENT stay, though, which was largely spent in Greenwich, Connecticut, I longed with a great passion to be in the city. Because of the reversal of the seasons, many of the Southern Hemisphere foreign students had already finished high school, and most of us had begun at the university. But even if I hadn't—even if I'd been a bona fide high school student, fifteen or sixteen years old, I'd have longed to spring myself from school.

I've never been able to warm to an institution—not school, and not marriage either, once I got there. I might have known this then. I did know it. I knew, too, that I was miscast in the role of "daughter" in a family of strangers. But, longing so fiercely to be lifted away from home, I'd set all this knowledge aside and taken part, together with my parents, in the fiction that the trip was to be heroic in its proportions.

To this end, my mother, against all suggestions to the contrary by the American Field Service—lists of clothing

appropriate for school, for the weather, for America itself—
had togged me out as if for a grand European tour. And so,
climbing down the steps of the plane at Idlewild in coat and
hat and gloves—looking and feeling, at eighteen, more like a
woman of thirty—I'd been in no sense ready for the year of
hail-fellow and high school and hootenanny that lay ahead.

But what to do about it, now that I was there? How to
spring myself, ensconced as I was in a high school, where
I was subject to bizarre rules requiring a permission slip
just to leave class and go to the lavatory, let alone leave the
premises to jaunt into New York? I may as well have been in
Idaho for all the fact that New York was so out of reach, and
the weeks passing into months, and all I'd go home with
would be a diploma I didn't need and the fictions I kept
writing to my parents in the form of letters.

Every day, I wrote an aerogramme, laboring now for
the spirited, heroic tone of those first letters from New
York. Each letter, I knew, would be read and reread before
being flourished around at the family on a Friday night.
How could I let my parents down in the face of this? How
could I let myself down, either?

And so, on I clacked, day after day, on the Olivetti—I
was taking typing at the high school, something I'd never
have learned in South Africa—jaunty, jocular letters that
never mentioned the crippling homesickness that afflicted

me from time to time, or the weight I was putting on, diving into the fridge for the exotica I'd discovered there—Sara Lee cherry cheesecakes, Pepperidge Farm apple turnovers, and so forth.

Recently, while cleaning out my garage, I came across boxes of these letters and settled in to read them. But after a few pages, I was finding them unbearable myself as well— all that noise, all those lies, all that sadness unrevealed. And the odd thing is that my mother, a reader with almost perfect pitch, did not question me. I take this as testament to her fierce desire to show off. Or, perhaps, for once, she just didn't notice. Or didn't want to. Or did, but was fearful I'd throw it all up and come home and disgrace them all. Which I might well have done were I not as averse as I am to abandoning a failure.

And good thing that I didn't, because, all at once, some months in, things began to look up. It happened this way: one morning, in a wild surge of inspiration, I sauntered into the school administrator's office and told him I was needed at the UN for a few days, and could he please sign me a slip? Had I rehearsed these lines—had I even mulled over the possibilities of how to set myself free—I'd probably have failed hopelessly. But, as it was, I stood before him, almost convinced myself of the truth of my petition. And when he signed me the slip, I wasn't surprised then either.

And so began my real adventure with America. For the rest of the year, whenever I could get away from school—a day here, a few days there—I'd take the one-hour train trip to Grand Central. My host family didn't seem to mind at all, and I'm still not sure they had any idea that I wasn't needed at the UN. No one ever questioned me except a UN guard, when I went there to watch a debate that was taking place on South Africa, and he was having none of it.

For three dollars a night I would stay in the dormitory at AFS headquarters, and no one there seemed to wonder why I kept turning up either. For another three dollars, I would buy a standing-room ticket at the old Met, and join the claque at stage left, taking in most of the season that way. Otherwise, I roamed the city, deliriously solitary in the thronging crowd, looking in at the shops, trotting into a museum, a concert, a symphony, happily racking things up to report home—for them, and for me, both. And then back I'd go to Connecticut, to fulfill at least some of the bargain I'd signed up for.

Part of the job of an exchange student, made clear to us from the start, was to foster international understanding. To this end, the four foreign students in the school would be carted off from time to time, either individually or as a group, to address another school, or a club—Rotary, Kiwanis, Elks, and so forth.

Before we left South Africa, AFS there had supplied us with all sorts of information for this purpose. In a mad show of zeal, they even arranged for us to be dropped a mile down a gold mine, and at such a rapid rate that our ears were in agony.

But, what I found, once I was on the circuit, was that talking about South Africa in the recommended way—its history and geography, a typical day in my schoolgirl life—only seemed to foster international boredom. As soon as question time came around, someone in the audience would ask, But aren't there lions where you live? Elephants? Tigers?

One day, a few months into this, the local AFS representative phoned to give me details for that night's event. It was to include the three other foreign students. "And, by the way," she added, "it's national dress."

National dress? I phoned the Dutch girl immediately. "What on earth are you going to wear?" I asked her.

She sighed. She had greater things on her mind. She'd come to America on an international Christian youth exchange program and had just discovered that she'd lost her faith. "I suppose," she said, "dat I ver dos vooden shoes, dat pointed hat, you know."

The enormous New Zealand girl had a sort of beaded grass skirt she was going to wear, and the Brazilian boy refused to consider anything beyond a Panama hat. But where did that leave me, a Jewish girl from a large South African city?

In desperation I asked my host "mother" for help. She was a woman completely at home in her own version of national dress—the lime greens and shocking pinks of Greenwich, Connecticut. As it happened, she thought for a bit. Then she looked up. "I know!" she said, leading me to a closet and pulling out a length of material vaguely resembling zebra. "Why don't you go as a Zulu?"

We were then at least a generation away from the first signs of political correctness, but even if we hadn't been, I'm not sure I wouldn't have leapt gladly at her suggestion. What was the alternative? To put a scarf over my head and go as Yentl of the South?

In the event, I arrived that evening barefoot and swathed in a sort of striped toga. I had my head in a turban, curtain rings hanging from my ears, and around my neck and wrists every piece of Zulu beadwork I'd brought to America to give away as presents.

I began my talk with elephants. We rode them to school every day, I said, and had to paint them different colors so that we could tell them apart. At school, we tied them up to parking meters, which they tended to pull up regardless, and, when school was over, we had to run around, finding them to ride home again, which happened to be up in the trees.

The Dutch girl was next. Every day, on her way to school, she said, she put her finger in the dyke. The New Zealand girl didn't go to school at all; she tended sheep and danced with Maoris. And the Brazilian boated down the Amazon to work on his father's coffee plantation. The evening was a wild success, and from then on we were in constant demand. We began to include singing, dancing, anything we could think of to spin the show as far from history and geography as we could get.

At my mother's suggestion, I wrote it all up for a South African newspaper, laboring hard over the timing, the details—which to include, which to leave out—condensing, altering, reshaping. It was an early exercise in transmuting life into life-on-the-page, and it hasn't got much easier since.

✳

IT IS OFTEN supposed that the writer wed to travel is a writer in search of the self. But the opposite is, perhaps, more true: the traveling writer is someone seeking anonymity. Or even a sort of nonexistence, the quest for which can lead, paradoxically, to the discovery of the self set free from the bafflement of context. "When are we more ourselves than when traveling?" asks Diane Johnson in *Natural Opium*. "The action of travel is all on the traveler—unless we happen to be carrying measles to the Amazon, or hard currency."

By extension, leaving home to live on the other side of the world can be a way of preserving home, as if in aspic, for our return. "A house is a good thing," an aborigine once said. "You can lock it up and go and live anywhere you please."

Once my AFS year was over and I'd returned home, I found myself both relieved and unsettled among all my beloved familiars. I certainly did not want to retrieve the year just over, but what I did begin to long for, in the mode of the newly liberated, was some sign that I'd be able to leave again when I was ready to do so. And then—life tending to deliver the solution to which one is equal to—I met a South African who was soon to leave for America, and who, once he was set up there, sent a breezy note to the effect that he had tickets for the Boston Symphony, and did I want to join him?

It's never a good idea for someone with captivity phobia to marry, or, at least, to marry young, to marry conventionally, and to do so largely, it seems to me now, as a gift to anxious parents. Still, this is what I did, charmed by the breeziness of that note into imagining a life conducted with just such a light touch.

But first I balked a bit. After a few weeks in Boston—a city I've never been able to warm to since—I found the lightness replaced by the sober prospect of the bargain I was about to make. So I phoned home.

"I'm having doubts," I said pathetically.

"What doubts?" My parents were worried themselves, I knew. They didn't want me returning to the man I'd left behind in South Africa, someone they considered altogether unsuitable, and who, not incidentally, wouldn't have dreamed of springing himself or anyone else from there and into the real world.

"I don't want to be stuck," I said, "and I want to travel."

My mother laughed. "For God's sake!" she boomed across the airwaves. "When are you going to come to grips with your itchy feet?"

As mixed metaphors go, this one had power, carrying, as it did, both the horror of life as a bag lady and the seduction of serious intentions—a husband, a child, a house, and all sorts of weighty things to put into that house. But, even so, I was miserable at the prospect. What I still wanted— what I had wanted since ever I could remember—was the vague delight, climbing onto that bus on Forty-second Street, of being a stranger in a strange place. Someone just arrived, just about to leave, and always with somewhere to go home to.

Had I thought of myself then as a writer, I might have been able to justify this restlessness, taken heart when James Salter said that travel is a writer's true occupation, that "a writer is an exile . . . and it is part of his life to keep on the move."

But he hadn't said that yet, and, even if he had, I wouldn't have felt justified in applying it to myself. Certainly, I'd been writing more or less since childhood—poems, stories, plays—but in the world I came from, such efforts were considered practicing, like scales on the piano, and were not to be taken seriously. Even in graduate school, once I got there, I found that the ambition to be a writer was considered presumptuous, at least in English departments.

So I continued to write as I'd always written, privately, and in my spare time. Looking back on this now, I think such an apprenticeship is by no means a bad thing. All those hours and years of struggle, conducted in solitude and without an audience, allowed me to build up a bit of muscle on the page before subjecting others to what I'd produced. At the very least, I was spared any number of rejections for work not ready to be published. And at worst, I had to engender my own hope.

Hope is, perhaps, more essential to a writer than luck. And yet, paradoxically, so is hopelessness. "One of the things I've discovered about writing," says E. L. Doctorow, "is that you have to sink way down to a level of hopelessness and desperation to find the book that you can write." So be it. But then, once you have found that book, if you have, you must rise again to some level of hope in order to be able to get on with it. And even then, there are lapses into doubt and despair. Whoever said that writing was a cheery business?

"No matter what I say," writes Marguerite Duras, "I will never discover why one writes and how one doesn't write . . . To be without . . . the slightest idea for a book is to find yourself, once again, before . . . [a] vast emptiness . . . something terrible, terrible to overcome."

Six years into marriage, my degrees behind me, and with a child, and a teaching job introducing a class of restless Vietnam vets to Shakespeare and Jane Austen, I was in a state of what I now recognize to be a sort of walking despair. I was stuck, as stuck as I had ever been—more stuck, of course, because what was there now even to hope for that wouldn't undermine someone else's life?

It is no coincidence that, with rare exceptions— Gertrude Stein, for instance, Edith Wharton, Jean Rhys, Rebecca West—most traveling writers were men. I don't mean to jump onto a soapbox here, but this is simply the case. Consider Bruce Chatwin, traveling writer extraordinaire. Here was a man wed to the idea of human restlessness and able to act on it without a backward glance. "Why do men wander rather than sit still?" he wanted to know, and then chased off to Patagonia, or to the deserts of Australia, for an answer. Once home, he'd settle into some friend's comfortable house to write. "Being away from his own address—wherever that might be—came to be a condition of his writing," writes Susannah Clapp in *The New Yorker*. "He produced much of his third book . . . in Wales, but had a breakthrough only when he went to Yaddo."

Where, of course, he was wonderfully looked after.

And bully for him, I say. Envy is not a sin from which I normally suffer. But show me someone free to go here or there, and I find myself singed by its fires. Still, at that point I didn't know much of Chatwin, and I had no idea of Yaddo either. I was in a veritable spider's web of looked- and looking-after—not only husband and child, but also the streams of South Africans, including parents and parents-in-law, who would come and stay for days or weeks, or even months. Pathologically restless, I found myself swooning with desire to move on once they had finally left. Even a short trip down the Amazon would have stilled that longing. At least for a while.

But the husband, who, before I'd met him, had sailed down the Congo himself, flown with his father around southern Africa in a single-engine plane, now began to embrace phrases like "discretionary income" and "fiscal responsibility." His idea of travel, I discovered, was two weeks at a family camp in some mountains near the Bay Area. It was a place run by the university he worked for, and there we went.

We were accommodated in a cabin with a sort of tent-like roof, and took our meals, kibbutz style, at long tables—some for adults, some for children. Every day, the children were herded into groups and led away to acquaint themselves with the wonders of Nature. The adults could choose their own groups. There was sailing or hiking or volleyball or pottery or macramé.

I've never been much good at Group, so I tried Sitting on Steps of Cabin with Book. This, however, also had its drawbacks. I found it hard to breathe, for instance. However much I tried, the air wouldn't go deeper than my shoulders. The camp was dusty. Dust billowed as you walked. It lodged in your clothing, up your nostrils, between your teeth. The camp doctor looked and listened. Then he let his stethoscope drop. "It has nothing to do with the dust," he said. "You're suffering from unhappiness. I suggest you go home."

It was at about this point that I asked myself a question I'd been asking most of my adult life: Is this what you want? Is this what you really want? Well, no, of course it wasn't, that much I'd known from the start. But not until now had I been able to come up with a real answer: what I wanted, what I had always wanted, was to write and to travel, as simple as that. And, suddenly, now I knew how I would accomplish this.

As soon as the quarter was over, I resigned from my teaching job (nothing heroic here: I was simply filling in for a professor enjoying a nervous breakdown). At home there was a struggle, of course—accusations and counter-accusations, doors slammed, terrible sulking by the Family Vacationer. Having grown up with a mother prone to much more inspired sulking, however, I was inured to its manipulations. And, anyway, I quite understood his point of view. Who, in a marriage, would want to see the other act out a dream of freedom that doesn't include himself? Certainly not he, and not I either, had the tables been turned. But they weren't, and, for the first time in years, I was full of hope.

What I did was to become a travel agent. I learned how to write a ticket from Kalispell to Nairobi—computers were not yet running things—and to work out minimum connecting times between the airports in Milan, and where to find a walking tour of Patagonia. It helped that I could work part-time, mostly from home, 8 to 10 a.m., after which I'd switch off the phone and go into what used to be the laundry but was now my studio. It was, for the time being, as far away as I could get.

Still, it was far enough to deaden the deafening cacophony of the house: Wash me! Fold me! Answer me! Tidy me! Fix me! Prepare me! Answer me! Cook me! Answer me! Now! As often as not, of course, I was to blame for listening. But, wed to order, I'd find myself thinking, "I'll just fix this, do that, and that, and maybe the other thing, and then it'll be done and I'll be free to work." Lives can pass this way; certainly unwritten books do.

But even with people to help—a servant, a devoted husband—Virginia Woolf exulted in their absence. "I have three entire days alone," she wrote, "three pure and rounded pearls."

In her memoir *Pen to Paper*, Pamela Frankau describes the enviable success of a fellow writer, whose pipe dream had materialized when a windfall allowed him to buy a house. And he would live there, he said, "'like a monk in a cell.' It is by all accounts a beautiful cell," writes Frankau. "Those who visit him return in envious raptures. They describe his study; they describe his garden; they talk of the lake and the trees and the silence. They tell me he has the perfect housekeeper and the kind of effortlessly wonderful secretary you read about in novels. But the last time I heard of him he was building himself a cottage at the end of the garden to get away from the house."

For me, those two doors between the laundry and the kitchen provided sufficient remove to write three novels and a number of short stories over a period of about five years. Interspersed with this—integral to it, I think—was the hope, the jazz, the lift that came with the travel I'd begun in earnest. I didn't ask myself why I had not granted myself this sort of permission before. "Granting oneself permission" to act out one's selfish desires is an invention of the psychological arts. One grabs, one doesn't grant, although if it makes one feel better to play both granter and grantee, so be it. It is interesting to know, perhaps, that the word *leisure* itself comes into English from the Old French, *leisir*, to permit.

This is not to say that the writing leapt easily and truly onto the page. On the contrary, I labored over any number of mediocre stories and two teething novels before finding, by chance, the way into my own subject. But, long before that, before even beginning my first novel—before the laundry, before the travel—I'd been sending out stories, and when they came back with their "having-given-your-material-careful-considerations" and "doesn't-quite-fit-our-editorial-needs," I hadn't allowed myself to despair for long; I had just sent them out again. As long as I was sending them out, there was something to hope for, like a win at the lottery. And still it was an exhausting game to play.

But then one day, in had come an acceptance note from a magazine called *Our Little Friend*. They had accepted a children's story I'd written about a girl who longs for a guinea pig, is given a guinea pig, loses the guinea pig, and then finds the guinea pig again. (Reduce any children's story to its plot and it could land up sounding almost as idiotic.)

Nine months later, my two free copies arrived, together with a check for ten dollars. For a while I just stared at the cover in wonder, savoring the sight of my name in print. But then I sat down to read the story, trying to pretend I was coming upon it for the first time. And just as I was thinking, Everything sounds better in print, even my children's story, there was Jesus. In an invasive editorial flourish, someone had inserted Him into the story, with the girl on her knees imploring Him to care for her lost guinea pig. And then there He was again in the closing sentence, once the guinea pig was restored, the story wrapped up neatly with a lesson: "And she was certain that Jesus heard a little girl's evening prayer."

In outrage, I wrote to the editor, and, in due course, back came his weary reply. *Our Little Friend*, he informed me, reserved the right to edit manuscripts with a religious slant, which I might have known for myself if I'd bothered to read their "Suggestions for Contributors." What's more, the press had been publishing *Our Little Friend* since

1890 and weren't about to change their policies for me. Investigating further, I discovered that *Our Little Friend* is published for use in the Sabbath schools of Seventh-day Adventists. So that was that.

✱

IT WAS TWO years after my *Our Little Friend* experience that I went off to my first and last writing conference, urged on by the fact that my first novel had been accepted for publication. I was now fairly desperate for the acquaintance of other writers. More than this, I wanted to know what it would be like to be part of the writing world. The novel had been sold by an agent, someone sufficiently new at the game to take on a writer with only *Our Little Friend* to her name.

The novel was a sort of upbeat, feminist story, quite common in the early eighties when women were liberating themselves all over the place. (As it turned out—did the curse carry over?—the publishers changed my title without permission and produced a paperback original that looked completely unlike its contents. It looked like a coy Harlequin romance with the following printed across the chest of the beauty on the cover: "The probing, moving novel that asks the question: How much is too much for a woman to want?")

But fortunately for me the novel wasn't yet published

when I arrived at Bread Loaf, where, over dinner one evening, Gail Godwin asked me, casually, what my novel was about. When I told her, her face fell. Why? she wanted to know. Why on earth was I concerning myself with American middle-class marital arrangements when I had a whole world of my own to write about?

When it comes to writing, I have always found questions more useful than comments. And, really, I had no answer for her except to say that I had tried to write about my world, tried and failed because it was the same thing, really—I'd been trying to write what everyone else was writing, subject and portent, and what had emerged was standard stuff, coming from no deeply felt or known experience of my own. More than this, I'd had no idea how to do it any other way, not until that very year when I'd found my way into a short story, just completed. And even then I hadn't seen how close I'd come to my own subject before she'd actually asked me that question.

If, as Pasteur said, "chance favors the prepared mind," my mind, without my even knowing it, had been preparing for her question for years. In fact, versions of it had been asked me many times before, but I had shrugged them off; I wasn't ready to find the answer. And so I'd turned to subjects that seemed more accessible—the America I knew (which, as it turns out, didn't go that deep either).

Someone once gave me what turned out to be a very good piece of advice: if you want to know what to write, ask yourself what obsesses you. Assuming one is lucky enough to have an obsession, there is first the question of recognizing it. Obsessions tend to live with us so naturally, there in the bloodstream, that even if we do recognize them, they can be too familiar to seem worth bringing out into the light. Whatever the case, Gail Godwin's question awoke in me an awareness of what might otherwise have taken me more years, and, if I was lucky, another book, to come to, if ever—my subject, my voice, my story. And I owe almost everything I have written since to that moment.

A theory seems to have resurfaced recently that to become a success at anything, one needs to devote about ten thousand hours to the practice of it. That is to say that if you write four hours a day, seven days a week, fifty-two weeks a year, you'd take about seven years to reach a professional level of efficiency. So be it; no surprise in this. Seven, fourteen, twenty-one years are going to go by whether one writes or not.

But what about chance? Where does chance feature in all this? Consider the understudy waiting in the wings, ready after her years and years of practice for the diva to come down with a sore throat on opening night. Again and again this is the way singers, actors, dancers make it into the light. In the writing world, there are other ways. One may not know, for instance, what face or force or direction, if any, will be put to a purpose such as mine was in going to that conference. And yet, as it turned out—and even though I lasted only forty-five minutes in the workshop itself—attending the conference was one the luckiest things I've ever done in my writing life. Certainly, I came away with what I'd gone for in the first place—a literary acquaintance, a sense of legitimacy. But nothing I had anticipated could have led me to imagine the chance of that dinner, that conversation, that question asked that sent me home to myself.

As soon as I returned, I began on my third novel, setting it aside now and then to hit the road. If a chance came up to bolt—a week in Egypt or a trip to Peru—I'd start my song and dance at home. The task was to invent a reason for leaving that would have my Family Vacationer feeling less left behind. He felt that, anyway, of course—he wasn't stupid—but, somehow, the song and dance seemed necessary nevertheless. In a sense, I suppose, we were both required to take part in the fiction that there was a weightier purpose to the travel than the travel itself. So I came up with all sorts of incredible reasons for spending a night on top of Machu Picchu, or floating down the Nile on a felucca, or spending three days at the Copacabana Palace in Rio.

None of this travel was particularly daring, much of

it shallow and predictable tourist stuff. But for me it was as if I had taken to opium. Best of all, perhaps, were the cruises. They weren't on the old steamships, alas, but still, there was the sea, the sight and the smell and the sound of it, the coastline out of reach, and the peace of the cabin to write in. No buses, no airports, no taxis, and almost no one, I found, to whom I'd want to talk.

A cruise to anywhere would do. And often I took the same route several times. I've recently discovered that I'm not alone in this. Mention a cruise, and the chances are that some writer will admit, rather sheepishly, to the addiction himself. I can think, offhand, of three of the least likely writers one would imagine who routinely take cruises.

And then there are the train people. I happened to spend much of my youth on trains, taking the seventeen-hour journey from Durban to Johannesburg, where I was at university, and then back again. These were the old-fashioned, wood-paneled trains, with green leather seats that, at least in second class, turned into six bunks. There were usually five or six of us students in a compartment, dinners in the dining car, tablecloths and silver and conductors flirting if they could get away with it. And then there were the parents left behind on the platform, the parents waiting there again when we came home for the holidays. A rehearsal, in my case, for the future.

A few years ago, I took one of those trains across South Africa, but now it had been tarted up for tourists by an entrepreneur, each compartment done out magnificently, with a proper bed, and a bathroom en suite, world-class dining, and, when I was on it, a jolly group of apple growers from Washington State. Had I been a train person, I might have felt more keenly the loss of the real thing. But, unlike cruise ships—every bit as far from the romantic utility of the old steamships as this train from the ones I'd taken as a girl—it produced no lift now to the heart, no enchantment to the distance between here and there as it crawled across the country.

As to the writing, it took place between trips and, very occasionally, during. And yet, somehow, the marriage of travel and writing worked well, although each seemed to have little to do with the other beyond that familiar balance between the liberation of departure and the writing to come home to.

I did discover a few things on the road that might have opened my eyes to the impulse behind my fiction. But they didn't. One was that, wherever I was, I tended to rearrange the furniture. Had the beds and chairs in the train compartment not been nailed down, I'd have moved them about there, too. Certainly I did that in hotels, and even an airline seat offers a few possibilities, particularly in first class, which is how I traveled when I worked as a travel agent, at a fraction of the price, of course.

Days or weeks before a trip, I'd start the preparations at home, shutting down the writing at a point at which I could take it up again, and then cooking and freezing and labeling, drawing up flowcharts in several colors, tripling my share of carpool and child swap. I've always prided myself on being low on guilt, but when I consider those years now, I see that this is a vanity.

Whatever the case, every time I left, I'd be assaulted afresh by the illegitimacy of the trip itself. Driving away from the house, I'd suffer a loss of breath, a clutch at the heart as I caught a last glimpse of the small face at the window. And I'd want to turn back right then, to give up, to give in.

But I never did. Often, if I was going to South Africa, I'd take her with me, however loudly my Family Vacationer pointed out that home now was where we lived, here, in America. But in this he was dead wrong. Home for me was—and remains, even now that it no longer exists— what I had left behind. And then found again in my third novel, the one I wrote after Gail Godwin's question. Home, I knew, was the place and the people, my parents waiting at the fence as I climbed down from the plane. And if the heroics of return have, at last, ceased, it is largely because they are no longer there to take part in them.

It occurs to me now that, had I not had America to return to, I'd have found somewhere else. How, otherwise, was I to achieve the rhythm, the paradoxical balance, to my life that I had always longed for? And that I now counted on to engender the necessary hope? Here and yet there. Paired and yet single. Home and yet exiled.

As to home, it seemed only to expand with the trips I took there. I discovered the bush, for instance. Never, my AFS caper notwithstanding, had I actually seen wild animals in their natural habitat before. My parents, who used to go regularly to the bush themselves, and then on to Lourenço Marques for a bit of nightlife, would leave my sisters and me behind. We would only fight in the car, they said, and spoil it for everyone.

So, on one of my early trips home, I went off to the bush myself. And fell instantly in love. However far the experience from that of Hemingway or Markham, still, it was Africa as I'd never known it as a girl. Once my marriage was over—because, of course, it did end—and I was now working as a freelance writer, I'd solicit as many articles as I could to take me back to South Africa, and, if possible, into the bush. It was, I discovered, where I'd be most likely to find the sort of moment, impossible to create, in which, suddenly, one feels old in a place, as if one has been there always. I have felt this at the Dead Sea, and at the Victoria Falls, and on Machu Picchu, and on ships, often on ships. They are the moments straight out of childhood, the past undivided from the present—harmonious, powerful, potent.

"To see in order to know," writes Astolphe de Custine, the nineteenth-century French aristocrat, in the introduction to his splendid book, *Letters from Russia*, "Such is the motto of the traveler . . . But if curiosity causes me to wander, an attachment which partakes of the nature of a domestic affection brings me back."

In the end, perhaps it doesn't matter how cheap the trick that achieves the first escape. What does matter is the illusion of freedom that the escape brings—because, of course, it is an illusion, as much of an illusion as the freedom of the animals to roam beyond the borders of their reserves without being shot for trophies or aphrodisiacs. Even for a child such as I had been, rehearsing for the future by wandering off into the servants' quarters as to the outer reaches of Siberia, there was a sense of adventure, a loosening from the known that brought with it that paradoxical longing for what had been left behind.

"To become a writer," says V. S. Naipaul, "that noble thing, I had thought it necessary to leave. Actually . . . it was necessary to go back. It was the beginning of self-knowledge."

For the traveling writer—for me, sitting on the deck of a ship, or on a verandah in Zambia, forcing myself to sample a ghastly plate of crocodile in rosemary cream sauce because there it is, asking to be experienced—there is an unquestioned affinity between travel and adventure, travel and reverie, travel and self-knowledge. Playing stranger in strange places has certainly given me the perspective of other worlds from which to examine my own. But, more than this, estrangement itself has become a necessary ingredient of my life, and of my work.

If, as Kierkegaard claimed, travel is the best way to avoid despair, then perhaps that's what this has been all about, this lifelong quest. So that now, with the restlessness calming down a bit as old age approaches, I can rejoice in feeling more or less strange everywhere. And also more or less at home. Homesick for nowhere. Permanently displaced. Free to come and go at last.

Keeping Watch

Those who did not live before the Revolution
never tasted the sweetness of life.
—Charles Maurice de Talleyrand-Périgord

SINCE THE ENDING OF APARTHEID, IT HAS BECOME
commonplace among South Africans, particularly middle-
class whites, to mourn not apartheid itself, but the world
that passed with it, a world that predated its demise by at
least a hundred years. What they miss most keenly is the
safety they had enjoyed in that world—at home, on the
street, in the car. In its place now is a sort of civil anarchy,
replete with knives, guns, AK47s, that has many leaving
the country, and those who stay taking shelter behind high
walls and electrified fences, alarm systems, panic buttons,
and private security guards.

Not long ago, they point out, children were free to bi-
cycle around the streets and women to drive wherever they

wished, day or night. Cars could be parked without a guard to pay off. Restaurants didn't have to lock you in behind wrought iron gates. Even the vast numbers of poor were safer; just ask them how they cope with this siege of violence.

And yet violence was always implicit in South African life, and often explicit as well. If guns were scarce before the eighties, knives certainly were not. Knife fights, flick knives, stabbings, stabbings, stabbings—these were the daily fare of newspaper reporting during the fifties, sixties, seventies. And if they were largely confined to ne'er-do-wells and Africans, well we all knew it was only a matter of time before it was going to climb the hill to find us.

So, when our garden boy came home half dead one day, stabbed just under the heart, I stared down at the wound as into an omen. There it was, a dark, moist, oozing thing, no distinction between dark skin and dark blood, and the gleaming white rib at the heart of it. Even at the age of six or seven, I knew exactly what I was seeing: I was seeing the future. Except that, for us, there would be no chance of a doctor stitching up the wound. For us, the knife was going to be drawn deep across the throat.

Much of my childhood anxiety was spent concocting ways to save myself when The-Knife-at-the-Throat day actually came—where to hide, whom I could count on for help (the nanny, although top of the list, would, at least in theory, be part of the same knife-wielding rampage). We all knew how it would happen. One night, without warning, all our servants would rise as one, snatch up a knife from their various kitchens, and rush next door to slit some white throats. Turn around, and there, in the doorway, would be Josiah, the Sullivans' cook, eyes wild with dagga and their carving knife at the ready. Our own servants, we knew, would not be able to bring themselves to slit our throats. So, they'd go over to the Sullivans, or to old Mrs. Holmes on the other side. She was always complaining about the noise we made on the cricket lawn and wouldn't give back the balls we hit over the hedge. And so, in a sense, it would serve her right.

Meanwhile, I kept watch. On a Sunday afternoon, if Zulus were pouring down the hill on their way to their faction fighting, I would sit at the study window, keeping a firm eye on them. Many were dressed in traditional warrior regalia—skins and shells and headbands—and they jumped and whistled and shouted and shook their sticks in the air, whipping themselves up into a frenzy for the contest that was going to take place down on the soccer fields at the beach.

All it would take, I knew, was for one of them to leap our fence and come crashing through the bed of cannas for the revolution to start right here, at our house, never mind that that wasn't the way it was supposed to happen. It had happened already in Kenya with the Mau Mau, a phrase that could bring terror into the heart of anyone, let alone a frantic child checking behind the wardrobe before she could bring herself to leap onto the bed and under the covers.

And so, when I woke up one night to the sight of a strange man at the foot of my oldest sister's bed, I was sure it had begun, and that no amount of cunning was going to be able to save me. We were at a holiday hotel in the mountains, my sisters and I in one room, my parents in the other, and the door firmly closed between us.

I lay still as stone, moving only my eyes. My bed was lower than the others—a sort of camp bed, brought in by the hotel and wedged into a corner. All I could see from down there was the man's hat, and the way his head bent over my sister's bed. So, maybe he'd slashed her throat already, I thought, and was checking to see she was dead.

But then what if he wasn't a native? What if he was a Coloured and didn't even have a knife? Coloureds, we knew, weren't going to rise up against us because they were better off than the natives and wanted to keep it that way. Our Coloured housekeeper had a bedroom next to mine, and used the children's bathroom, and ate the same food as us, but in the kitchen, and off different dishes.

I took another look, but it was impossible to tell. In the dark he could even have been an Indian. An Indian had once lured a girl in my class into an alley, and he'd made her pull down her pants, and a nurse, leaning out of an upstairs window, had seen them down there and called the police. And after that the girl had seemed different, as if she had a birthmark down her face, or a limp, or a mother who had died.

But no one ever thought Indians would rise up and slit our throats either. They worked as waiters and gardeners and behind stalls at the Indian market. Some of them had shops down on Grey Street, and my mother knew them, and they knew her. Come the revolution, she said, the natives were as likely to slit their throats as ours. Everyone knew that natives hated Indians. When the natives had rioted against them and burned down their shops, a native had thrown a brick at my uncle, who was dark and looked a bit like an Indian himself. And when Pillay, our gardener, had to use the toilet in the servants' quarters, they weren't at all pleased, the house girl told me. Indians were dirty, she said, they stank of curry and hair oil, phew, and also they cheated you. Except that she called them *coolies*, a word we were never allowed to use.

The man glided to the foot of my middle sister's bed. Now that he was closer, I tried to sniff for curry or hair oil. But there was only the smell of the room—coir matting and furniture polish. And outside the crickets were singing as if everything were normal, the window was wide open as usual, never mind that we were on the ground floor, because however much they threw the phrase around, my parents were far more concerned about fresh air than they were about The Knife at the Throat. At home, the French doors onto the verandahs were fastened back day and night, upstairs and downstairs, the windows, too. But when I worried about this, they just pointed out that the only invaders we'd ever had were monkeys, which would reach into the kitchen to snatch something from the table, and then gibber up with it into the mango tree, the dogs in pursuit.

It was the dogs, really, that were meant to protect us. As long as they lay around our feet, cocking an ear for someone to chase—anyone, in fact, who didn't belong in the house—we were supposed to feel safe. Just let the garden boy emerge from the servants' quarters and they'd be after him in a pack, barking, snarling, snapping. The same held for Pillay, the Indian gardener, and for delivery boys, and for the Zulus pouring down the hill on a Sunday afternoon.

And yet what good were they now, here in a hotel in the mountains, with a man staring down at my middle sister? They were hundreds of miles away, at the kennels. And anyway, how many dogs would it take when all the servants rose up at once with their knives and sticks? Even Superman, our houseboy, had managed to slice Simba's ear with the stick he carried to protect himself between the kitchen and the garage, or back to his room in the servants' quarters. And when an enemy put a curse on him one day and he came to say he was leaving and wanted his wages, it was almost as if the dogs themselves were cursed, too, because they just stood back and watched as he walked to the gate, carrying his cardboard suitcase.

The man turned toward my corner. And just as I was thinking that, whatever he was, I would leap up before he could get to me and scream at the top of my lungs—just then, he turned and walked over to the window. I pushed myself up a bit to see, and, yes, there he was, climbing out, first one leg and then the other, and he was still wearing his hat.

As soon as he was gone, I jumped out of bed and burst through the interleading door into my parents' room. But they were too fast asleep to take me seriously. Eventually, though, my mother did climb out of her bed and led me back to my own, agreeing, for once, to close the window. And then, the next morning, as soon as I heard the early morning tea trolley rattling down the passage, I was back at their bedside.

And something about my insistence must have caught their attention at last, because, when he'd finished his tea, my father put on his dressing gown and slippers and came through to our room to question my sisters. They scoffed, of course—they'd seen nothing, heard nothing. But then, opening the window to let in some fresh air, he noticed some soil on the windowsill. And, when he leaned out, there, in the flowerbed below, were four large footprints— two on their way in and two on their way out. No one ever found out who or what the man was, and no one but me believed he could have had anything to do with The Knife at the Throat.

And so on we went, doors and windows open, dogs in place, until the real terror began—coming not at all as we'd expected, but haphazardly, here or there, day or night, with guns as well as knives, because by then guns were almost as plentiful and cheap as hamburgers, and the dogs themselves were the first to be shot—until then we carried on with the paradise of our lives: luxurious but not rich, safe and yet threatened, carefree if one did not think too carefully about the future.

Useful Zulu Phrases, 1986

WHITE SOUTH AFRICANS ARE CONVINCED THAT HAVing servants is no easy matter. They like to say that servants are like children. What they mean is that servants need watching. That they lack responsibility. And that their understanding is on a level with their English.

For an English employer, the servant who speaks English is indeed the best sort to have. But the tiresome fact is that servants grow up speaking their own languages. If they speak English at all, it is of a rather primitive variety. This clearly hampers the process of servanting. And there is the additional problem of knowing just how much English the servant understands. On the one hand, employers maintain that servants understand far more than they pretend to. And, on the other, that they have the infuriating habit of pretending to understand when they don't.

Just to make sure, an employer will usually follow an order with, "Do you understand?" To this question all servants nod. But then the Hoover turns up broken, or the white sauce comes out like glue, and where is a master or madam to turn next?

One might think that a solution lies in learning Zulu. But this is to ignore the difficulty English speakers have with foreign languages. And particularly with languages like Zulu, whose complexity seems to them to be in inverse proportion to that of its native speakers. Zulu is a language of strange sounds and clicks and whooshes far beyond the skills and dignity of most English speakers.

For the frustrated householder, there is help. *An Easy Zulu Vocabulary and Phrase Book: Simple Sentences for Use in the Home and Garden and on Other Everyday Occasions* is a small paperbound volume, first published in 1938 by Shuter and Shooter, an old and respected South African publisher of school books and other texts. Now in its fourth edition (1982, with new orthography), "the primary object [of the book]," says its preface, "is to help newcomers in their common contact with Zulus." Phrases of common contact are grouped under the headings *Gardening, Health, Housework, Motoring, Stabling, Store Work,* and *Miscellaneous.*

The beauty of this little book lies in the fact that, apart from a simple vocabulary list, most of the phrases of common contact are conveniently voiced either in the interrogative or in the imperative. If, for instance, one wants to know what to wear, there is the phrase for "Is it hot today?" If one has trouble hearing, there's "Always call me when the telephone rings." Offensive habits can also be done away with. "Do not touch anything," "Do not spit like that," and "Do not smear your clothes with blood" are a few of the phrases provided for this purpose.

For the talkative servant, one finds a trio of injunctions: "Be silent," "Be silent while I am speaking," and "You must not speak while another is still speaking." To deal with the tricky problem of encouraging one's servant's intellectual skills, while still maintaining household standards, there is the following sketch in the Miscellaneous section:

Can you read?
It is good to read.
You may go to school in the evening.
You must finish all your work first.
You must not neglect work for the sake of reading.
That is bad.
It is very bad to make learning an excuse for laziness.

✱

OFF-TIME ON SUNDAYS—ALWAYS a sticky point when hiring a servant who claims to be devout—can be solved with "If you go to church on Sunday, you must return in time to do what is necessary."

The hiring of servants itself is, in fact, a complicated matter. There are things an employer must know. If a cook is to be hired, what kind of cooking has been done before? "Plain cooking" (anchovy toast, Welsh rarebit, rock cakes) might suit one madam, but another may demand "Jewish cooking" (chopped herring, fried fish, and knowing which rag is meant to clean which dish). Standards differ too. So do duties, wages, hours.

An Easy Zulu Vocabulary provides some welcome relief. An employer can start off with a few standard phrases like "You will have to do any work that I tell you," "Do not make a noise in the evening," and "Come at once when the bell rings." And follow these up with such specifics as "You must get up at six," "Catch two young roosters," and "Cut their heads off."

Using this book, one can also lend one's servants to friends—"Go with the White man," "Go with the lady." Or have errands—difficult to communicate otherwise— carried out properly: "Take the master's food to the store" is followed by "Hold it carefully, that the gravy be not spilled."

"That the gravy be not spilled" demonstrates nicely one of the subtler points of master-servant dialogue. The quaint formality of the word order, the injunction against spilling (gravy here, rather than seed)—the whole tone of the message, in fact—is intended to communicate to the servant that God is speaking. A God somewhere between the fierce Old Testament Jehovah and the rather more benign New Testament Paternoster.

It is this role toward which the employer actively works, and which, in the end, tests the master-servant bond. If the white man is God, the reasoning goes, then the servant, like Abraham, can be tried. To effect.

A small picnic vignette, hidden in the Motoring section, demonstrates the point nicely:

We will stop here. ....*Sizokuma lapha.*
We will have some lunch. .... *Sizodla ukudla kwasemini.*
Make a fire. ....*Phemba umlilo.*
Put the kettle on. ....*Basela iketela.*
Spread the rug in the shade. ....*Endlala ingubo emthunzini.*
Get out the lunch basket. .... *Khipha ubhasikidi wokudla.*
See how deep the river is. ....*Hlola ukushona komfula.*

Gloria Mundi

SOMETIMES, AFTER MY DAILY DOSE OF RADIATION, I would stop at a small bath store near the hospital to buy a bar of soap, perhaps, or a bottle of bath gel. I liked the little shop; it was holding its own among the retro hippie emporia of the neighborhood, no hint yet of tea tree or patchouli or tie-dye.

Looking back on that time now, I wonder whether I was drawn to soaps and gels because unlike, say, a belt or a pair of shoes, they could be counted on not to outlast me. I don't know; I didn't go in search of a belt or shoes, and was in no mood then for metaphors of mortality.

Down in the radiation suite, beyond natural light, it was as if a scrim had been lifted, revealing a just perspective on everything. I would look with keen interest at the other victims, wondering whether, like me, they had come to a new understanding, an acceptance—at times, even a celebration—of the temporal nature of all things.

Which was not to say I had not always known that nothing lasts. My twelve years in an Anglican school in South Africa had built in daily reminders of the impermanence of the things of this earth. So, too, did the poetry we read, the histories, the Bible itself. I would listen, I would read, I would understand. And then, when school was over, I would go back into my life, feeling immortal.

Still, as a Jew, I rather envied Christians their faith in an afterlife. Every morning, in prayers, we sang hymns, glorious hymns, heaven all around us. "Everything shall perish away," sang our Zulu maid, daughter of a Methodist minister, with a lusty cheerfulness that made perishing away seem like joyful anticipation.

But for me, pedaling off to Hebrew school three afternoons a week, there was no such assurance. Jews, as I came to understand it, didn't pay much attention to heaven; when we died, it seemed, we disappeared. What did matter was to remember our earthly history, to observe our laws, and, never mind what the Almighty allowed to happen to us, to praise, glorify, exalt, and extol Him regardless—He-whose-name-was-so-terrible-it-was-never-to-be-uttered.

Meanwhile, my mind would wander away into the future, that time that seemed so slow in coming, when all this would be over, school and Hebrew school both, and I'd be free. But to be what, I would wonder. And where? And how? And even though I knew that the Almighty tended to smite those who disobeyed His laws, being smitten didn't worry me too much, sitting there on that hard bench with other fractious and smelly nine- and ten-year-olds, all of us worn out after a long day of it.

I would stare out of the window in what I took to be His direction and implore Him to get me through this and out into the real world as quickly as possible. If He did, I promised, I would praise, glorify, exalt, and extol Him every day of my life. Promise, promise, promise.

And then, out of nowhere, could come a thought to make my heart jump in terror: at any moment, death itself might snatch away my mother or my father. It had happened to others; it could happen to me. And for this even the thought of heaven would provide no comfort. I wanted both of them here, on earth, alive, and, if someone had to die first, I wanted it to be me. Then, at least, there would be no question of being left behind.

And so I kept a firm eye on them, taking comfort from their insouciance in the face of life's terrors as I saw them— doors left wide open to the night, windows, too—and even from the way my father drove, like a madman, cornering on two wheels, pushing the old DeSoto to 108 miles per hour on the open road.

When, finally, he did die, not in a car crash, but, at the age of eighty-five, from lung cancer, still I was left—quite adult now, quite mindful of mortality—more shocked, more desolate and bowed down than I might have been as a child. It was as if childhood itself had died with him, home as well—a childhood and a home that, without thinking, I had counted on to carry me through to the end.

Then, a year after his death, anomalies showed up on a routine mammogram. Biopsies followed, blood tests, MRIs, CT scans, X-rays, a lumpectomy, and six weeks of radiation. People who claim to know how one thing leads to another had no doubt of cause and effect: some were for the death of my father, others for a divorce I'd battled through some years before. Stress, grief, loss—these were the words invoked when laying blame for an illness whose cause was (and remains) unknown.

But grief is not a cigarette, and neither is stress. And none of the remedies offered by the grief-and-stress brigade—meditation, yoga, exercise, "mindfulness," supplements, diets of every description—none of these seemed able to turn me from a person who worried things through to someone who could take things as they came.

Nor, I found, my brush with mortality notwithstanding, was I to be transformed from someone who could take
pleasure in a bar of triple-milled French soap, and, over
time, in more enduring purchases—a pair of sandals, perhaps, linen sheets, an Indian miniature painted on ivory,
an antique ivory doctor's doll—into an ascetic, or at least
someone who would consider shopping trivial in light of the
greater scheme of things.

And if, once the radiation was over, the purchases I
began to make again were to outlive me, I could take pleasure even in this. In fact, the whole idea of transience took
hold of me like a sort of rapture. *Sic transit gloria mundi*, we
had learned in school. *Memento mori.* "Look on my works, ye
Mighty, and despair!" we'd recited. "Ah! *Vanitas Vanitatum!*"
we'd read, "Which of us is happy in this world? Which of us
has his desire? or, having it, is satisfied?"

And though, at the age of fifteen or sixteen, I understood
quite well the truth and scope of Thackeray's words, yet,
ambitious as I was and wild for life, I enjoyed an unquestion-
ing faith that the things I desired, both material and imma-
terial, would deliver a measure of satisfaction. Satisfaction,
delight, hope—even the choosing of a new pencil box at the
start of a school year could bring fresh immediacy to life.

It was with just such hope that, more than forty years
later, the radiation treatments behind me, I went in search

of something new to wear for an upcoming book tour. What I wanted was a change of look, something in keeping with the wisdom I thought I'd acquired during the soap-buying times. The writing of the book itself had straddled the long vigil over my father's dying, and I had finished it just before the offending mammogram. So now, a year later, there I was again, with what felt like familiar purpose, back at the racks, the shelves, the dressing rooms of desire.

My mother had practiced just such purposefulness when she was out on a hunt, clipping along in her stockings and heels, mouth set, watch consulted, as if the whole business of shopping were to be put behind her with dispatch so that the real work of the day—a play to stage, a cast to assemble—could begin.

But she didn't fool me. I knew perfectly well that shopping was work, too, joyful work. To search among the limited offerings available in a far-flung country—to go in search, say, of an evening dress in which to take a bow, something classic that would endure when the fashions changed, or a good pair of Italian shoes, ditto, Sanderson linen for the lounge curtains that had perished in the sun, and, if there was time, to hurry down the lane to the little antique shop where Mr. Potts, who lent her props for her stage productions in return for an ad in the program, might be persuaded to lower the price on a lovely Georgian cigarette box, because how many years had they known each other? she would ask him, and then turn away to examine a pair of silver grape scissors so that he had time to consider—to spend a morning like this, and then come away in triumph, was to breathe the very oxygen of life.

The fact is, objects of desire have always seemed to bring with them what I can only think of as promise for the future—not only in the having, but also in the seeking, of them. And if the search produces nothing, or if, once something is found, the promise turns to dust after a day or so, well, still there has been the sport of it, the anticipation, the pounce, the triumph over the deadening brake of common sense.

And yet, having made it back onto a real shopping street after all those months of abstinence, I felt as if unmoored. There I stood in front of a three-way mirror, trying too hard to love the look of myself in a breathtakingly expensive designer suit. I had chosen it over all natural inclination, but, somehow, the new way of seeing life had left me unable to see myself in any familiar way. Or even to dismiss the saleslady's loud approval, which would once have left me untouched.

"Understated," she said, circling, "timeless." And, staring at myself in the three-way mirror, pale and rather thin, I wished, oh I wished that my mother were not old and demented, or, even if she were, that her astral spirit were there to say to me, "Darling, take it off, it makes you look like an undertaker."

But she was not there, and, forgetting completely that I had never warmed much to understatement, and certainly not to the timelessness of mud green, I bought the suit, and wore it a few times during the book tour in the spirit of a cross-dressing undertaker. And then, when the tour was over, I retired it to the back of my wardrobe, where, happily, moths found it, making it easier to throw out when the time came. And although the times for throwing out began to bank up more regularly—to take hold, in fact, as a sort of ideal—on the shopping streets themselves I was returning to myself. Strolling in and out of the shops, it was as if I'd never suffered any sobering reminders of perishing away for all the rapidity with which hope could return at the sight, say, of a cheerfully lined basket, marked down now because the overpriced little French boutique was going out of business.

I stared at it. Another basket? Was I not already rich in baskets? But if I was, so what? Almost every night now I woke in panic, 2 a.m., 3 a.m., alone in the darkness. *Timor mortis conturbat me*, I would tell myself. And then, Yea, though I walk through the valley of the shadow, etc.

So, what, in the greater scheme of things, could a French basket matter? This small pleasure? This brief dart of hope?

Nothing, that I knew. Standing there in the bright light of day, I reminded myself that summer was coming at last, I could use the basket to carry cutlery out into the garden when friends came for lunch. Or I could go to France myself. Or to Italy. Or to Greece. I could install myself on my favorite Greek island. Already I could imagine the view down to the Aegean. Already, sandals were perching in shoe-store windows like brightly colored swallows. And the long grey winter was almost over.

Multiple Choice

THE IDEA OF BEING LOCKED INTO A CHOICE—A JOB, A marriage, an airline ticket—has always sat like a boulder on my breathing. Terror of regret infects not only the choice to be made, but also the choices to be left behind. Going, I want also to have stayed. Spending, I want still to have the money.

And yet, paradoxically, I am prone to making rash choices. Only let someone say, "You are an adventuress," and I am off, looking for adventure. Let a virtual stranger suggest that I may be tied up with the wrong sort of man, and I am instantly considering a blueprint for another. Some years ago, on the strength of a friend saying, "If I were you—", I bought a house in a small town, miles from the city I had lived in for twenty years. No sooner had I settled into my new house, though, than I began to consider what people had been telling me since I first came to America: "You belong in London."

As it happens, I am at my most suggestible on the subject of belonging, probably because I am not much good at it. And so, being told with casual authority that I belong in London tends to make me forget, for the moment, that I have never been able to feel at home in the place. One thing I do love about London, however, is the friends who live there. And so, when the airfares to London plunged one fall, I decided, on a whim, to go and see them. Or, more precisely, to go and talk to them. Talking with them all together there, would, I hoped, put the matter of London to rest once and for all. Face to face, perhaps, we would solve my life.

As soon as I had made the reservation, however, spending one thousand dollars for a conversation with friends began to seem frivolous. So did flying eight thousand miles for only a week. When I mentioned this to a local friend, she said, Why go then? Why indeed, I thought. My ticket only had to be purchased at the airport. Suddenly, I felt gloriously reprieved from a life of bagladyhood.

But then, thanking her, hanging up, I immediately began to mourn the trip not yet canceled. What, after all, was one thousand dollars in the scheme of things? A visit to the dentist? A repair to the roof? I phoned my friend back and told her this, reminded her of the time, twenty-five years before, when a man had made me choose between a trip to Europe and marrying him, and I had chosen the trip. And then, two days later, terrified of regret, had unchosen the trip and married him after all. And then, eighteen years later, had unmarried him, and here I was, no wiser.

Honor your instinct, she said. For the next few days, I carried the phrase around with me, wondering, Which instinct? Go or stay? Bury yourself deeply enough in ambivalence and you become deaf to instinct. Or, perhaps, instinct itself dies of suffocation. And so you are forced into a pretense of rationality: on the one hand, on the other hand. I have lain awake at 3 a.m., feeling rationally imperiled by the purchase of a pair of shoes. I have bought and sold houses, accepted jobs at the other end of the continent and not suffered quite so acutely. Somehow, there are times when choice, any choice, can bring one's whole life to bear on the choosing. And this was one of them.

Four days before leaving, I was still casting about for a decision, consulting anyone I could find to listen. I realized that, depending on what answer I wanted, I phrased the question accordingly. If I wanted a yes, I talked of conversation among women, carpe diem, the London theatre, the British Museum. If I wanted a no, I talked of money and time, or I admitted that I didn't really love London, certainly not as a place to live. Italy, perhaps, or Greece— somewhere warm for half the year, and then, maybe, New York or San Francisco for the other half.

In the meantime, all impulse was draining from the trip itself, all possibility of whim, all charm. I knew I was carrying the matter over the edge of sanity, trying the patience of my friends, but I couldn't help myself. I even developed a toothache and decided I couldn't go. Then, the day before departure, it went away again and I changed my mind. But still I hadn't packed. Finally, I called the airline to cancel. That, I thought, would take the matter out of my hands. "At this fare?" the agent cried. "Are you sure? I even bought a ticket myself!"

On the way to the airport, I stopped downtown to have lunch with the one friend who knew nothing of the madness that had afflicted me. She would, I thought, give me a fresh perspective on the subject. Sitting in her office, considering her settled life—a husband, two children, a real job—I was embarrassed to admit my predicament. But all the way into town, I had been thinking that it still wasn't too late to cancel. Help me, I said to her. Tell me what to do.

She stared at me in disbelief. Look, she said, waving her hands around the cubicle. See what I'm stuck in? See this? See this?

I looked around at the slick machinery of office life, the nine-to-five-ishness, the sealed-in, white-on-white, no-choice road not taken. And I carried the image with me onto the plane. There, settling back into the fait accompli of the journey, I found ambivalence receding with a glass of wine, thirty thousand feet above the ground.

By the time I sat with my friends, high on Hampstead Hill, it had vanished completely. We talked on and on, around and around the predicament of the friend who had moved there recently, but who thought she might still belong in New York. House, job, men, money—there she was, smiling apologetically, soliciting our opinions. I heard the way she phrased and rephrased her questions. I saw the way she heard some answers and not others. On the one hand, she said, on the other . . .

Letter from London

I HAVE COME TO LONDON TO ESCAPE "JINGLE BELLS" and "O Holy Night" in the shopping malls of Texas. But Harrods has been worse, far worse. It has been warfare. And now I make my way to Paddington like a refugee, find the Oxford express, squeeze myself into a standing space, already crowded, between two railway carriages, and lean back against the toilet door.

I am still jetlagged—something I shall have to account for to the Oxford don who has invited me to his college feast tonight. We are new friends, and so I have had to pretend to take his jetlag diet seriously. Weeks before I left, it arrived in the mail. No normal food thirty-six hours prior to departure, going to bed in the middle of the afternoon, nothing but water on the plane—that sort of thing. I have taken no notice at all. To me, the English themselves seem jetlagged. Four o'clock in the afternoon and they are already half asleep.

"BREE-BRAY-OO-RWEEGWTZ-O-RAA—"

British Rail regrets a delay, that much I work out. The English regret; Americans apologize. Americans forbid; the English request. In the pastry department of Harrods is a sign requesting shoppers not to eat their purchases on the premises. Americans eat anything they like anywhere at all—as long as it isn't washed down with alcoholic beverages, which are forbidden.

"Sodding British Rail and their bloody 'inclement weather'!" a man growls under his breath.

I fan my ticket around my nose. Someone has farted. The air is heavy with bad breath, and with years of masculine sweat recycled occasionally through British dry cleaning. There's no saving the dress I'm carrying in a garment bag over my arm. It's been carried all over London. It can't be ironed; it must be steamed. I wonder whether there'll be somewhere to hang it over a bath. Whether there'll be a bath at all. Or heating. Or a plug for the hairdryer. The College, my don has informed me, was built in the thirteenth century. I am to be housed in the Fellow's guest room, in one of the turrets.

A knocking starts up behind me. The WC door pushes open a crack.

"I say," comes a plummy woman's voice from within, "I'm not actually using the convenience, you know. I'm just sitting on the lid—"

The man next to me wakes up, clears his throat, and stares down at his shoes. No one smiles. You'd never imagine from this lot how the English cripple up with laughter over mention of the simplest toilet functions.

"What I mean to say is that if anyone needs to use the convenience—"

"BREE-BRAY-UNN-BATCHAH—"

A whistle sounds, and we're off, lurching and swaying out of Paddington and into the darkness of a winter afternoon.

In Oxford, my don is waiting anxiously on the platform, just where he said he would be. He rolls up my garment bag into a compact cylinder and places it under his arm like a newspaper. He is Oxford's Big Bang man and looks the part— long grey hair growing in every direction, steel-rimmed glasses, crooked teeth, a patch of beard at the chin, missed by this morning's shave. He offers me his elbow and heads off into the rain and wind with his umbrella at an angle.

My room, as it turns out, is almost modern—which is to say it has a portable heater, a plug, hangers, and a bathroom. Next to the bed, instead of a Bible, is a history of the college, 1263–1939. I page through it while the bathroom fills up with steam. By the time I hear my don's rat-a-tat-tat, I am bathed and dressed, ready for an evening of high table talk and ancient ceremony.

But, when I open the door, I find him quite transformed. He has pulled his hair back into a ponytail. He's wearing a doublet and hose, silver buckles on his shoes, frills at his neck and wrists. He has even applied some rouge.

"Good God!" he cries, clapping one hand over his brow. "Didn't I tell you it was fancy dwess?"

I shake my head, considering, for a few mad moments, the possibilities of the bedspread and a bath towel. But he has recovered and is offering me his arm, leading me down the winding, mediaeval stairs to meet the others for champagne in the Senior Common Room.

When we arrive, the place is already alive with English at play. There are men dressed up as women—all boned into bodices, with beauty spots and lacy caps—men dressed up as men, with powdered wigs and canes; women in pantaloons and waistcoats; women in crinolines and bonnets. The scene is a cross between Monty Python and Masterpiece Theater.

"I believe," says a woman in a pointed cap, "that one can buy bits of the Berlin Wall at Harrods."

"Don't touch the goose if it's pink," my don whispers urgently in my ear. "And watch out for the oysters. Last year they were catastwophic."

At dinner I find myself seated between Sydney Carton and a man dressed up as George Sand dressed up as a man. Despite my woolen underwear, I am freezing. The dining hall is vast and ancient and built of stone. It seems to have its own weather system. There are breezes going one way around my feet and another around my neck. Chilled oysters are out of the question. In fact, it's almost too cold to talk. Anyway, Sydney Carton is talking to Emma Bovary on his left, and George Sand, for some reason, is scrutinizing my pearl choker.

"Princess Di?" he asks at last, with a sly smile.

Before I can answer, the chef comes in with a goose on a platter and presents it to the master of the college. We all applaud and it is carried out again, coming back carved up, quite brown, and semi-warm.

But then, as soon as the plates are cleared, everyone stands up as if on cue and moves to another dining hall, colder than the first, for dessert and cheese. I begin to flag. My oyster and goose companions have been seated elsewhere. I must begin again to make it clear that I am dressed, more or less, as myself—a visitor from America. And start again on discussion of one country versus the other. I want to go to bed. It is 5 a.m. in California, and there's coffee still to be had back in the Senior Common Room.

I glance around for my don. He is burying a yawn in the

frill of his cuff. His ponytail has come undone. A few hairs, however, still spring out of his elastic band, giving him the profile of a gaunt, beaked samurai. I give him a keen look, hoping we can leave.

In a flash, he's at my side. "I say," he purrs, "after coffee, I have some wather splendid Cognac in my wooms."

This takes me off guard. Until now, there has been no suggestion of anything between us, not even Cognac. Apart from anything else, he is a man with an extraordinary reverence for ill health. He has warned me against the damp, and told me of a special cream he uses for fungus growing between his toes. Alcohol, he claims, can bring on terrible headaches.

I touch my fingers to my forehead. There is something terribly unsexy about the English national speech defect of *w*'s for *r*'s. "I have rather a headache," I say.

Instantly his face comes alive with concern, or delight, or both. "The plum pudding!" he cries. "Full of animal fat! A simple matter of logical deduction!"

"Crispin," says Chopin, wife of George Sand, "are you giving your guest the lowdown on Harrods Food Hall?"

"Certainly not!" cries my don. "As far as I'm concerned, it's gone to pot since Al-Fayed took over."

"Hear! Hear!" says someone else, man or woman, farther down the table. "Frankly, I can't see the point of London at all these days, can you?"

✱

ON THE PLANE coming back, I am seated next to an Englishman, who, after three Scotches and a bottle of wine, confesses that he goes in for "non-penetwative" sex. Roger Vadim, he informs me, took three months before he could manage it with Jane Fonda—he'd just read his memoir. I glance out of the plane window, considering Englishmen in striped pajamas suggesting a "woll in the hay" to their lady wives. Or to their lady friends. Or, perhaps, to a friendly tart in the back of a taxi.

Back in California, I stand, half dead, at the baggage carousel next to a tall, tanned American in snakeskin cowboy boots and a cashmere jacket. His hair is thinning, and his ears stick out a bit, but he has lean hips and lovely, large, veined hands and is looking at me with interest.

"Just come in from London?" he asks. He's wearing a massive one-of-a-kind bright gold wedding ring—all crevices and peaks, with the head of the MGM lion roaring out of the middle of it.

I nod. Any day, red hearts will be showing up for Valentine's Day. And then there'll be Easter bunnies and ducklings and eggs. I was quite ready to leave London, but I'm not glad to be back. "I'm jetlagged already," I say to him.

He smiles down at me with black eyes and even teeth. "Only one way to beat jetlag, honey," he says, hanging his hands by the thumbs in the pockets of his jeans. "Fly first class."

Caveat Viator

I TURN SHARPLY OFF THE HIGHWAY, UP TO THE HOTEL, only to find my path blocked by a white Lexus. The couple inside gestures wildly at the bushy hillside. The man has a camera at the ready, the woman a pair of binoculars. I switch off my engine and wait. I am acquainted with this sort of behavior. It is practiced by game spotters in the African bush, sighting a leopard, a cheetah, a lion making a kill. What one can hope for, though, from a hillside in between Northern California's Route 1 and the Pacific Ocean, I can't imagine. A snake? A rabbit? Or some more endangered creature given sanctuary by the ecologically correct, New Age barons of the tourist industry who have built this place?

I start my car, tired of waiting. But just then two pointed ears appear above the grass and the couple is riveted. A doe and her faun trot out into the road, change their minds, turn back again, and disappear. The couple turns to me, triumphant. They smile. I smile back. To have lived in Northern California for twenty years is to be inured to the tyranny of Reverence. Its objects are legion—Nature, Being, Love, Self, Loss, Grief, Pain, etc. And now, of course, Our Planet.

At the reception area, I am offered herbal tea and instructed to abandon my car. An attendant in an electric cart drives me up the hill to the hotel itself. It is windy and cold up there, twelve hundred feet above the Pacific. Most of the hotel's clientele, the attendant informs me, come up from L.A. They come here to Replenish. A pair of them in thick terry robes glides past us down the path. They are smiling beatifically—not, it seems, at us or at even each other, but simply at Life. They are going, the attendant says, to the basking pool, which is open twenty-four hours a day, whenever the spirit might move you toward it. "In a place like this," he suggests ominously, "it is best to follow wherever the spirit moves."

As we buzz along the path, he points out certain guest rooms, built on stilts among the trees, others that look like bunkers, with sod roofs, buried in the hill. No trees were felled to build this resort, he points out. Not even the roots of the trees have been disturbed. In fact, there is a living bench made out of living trees from which to watch living bass swim around a pond. There is also a wedding palette near the edge of the cliff on which those who wish to do so can be married.

The attendant, I decide, would make an excellent New Age Brown Shirt. Apart from his earring, his uniform, his short-cropped blond hair, and his muscled, tidy body, he has perfected, in tone and delivery, a distinct air of moral superiority, an edgy hint of threat.

We stop outside a wooden structure built down the hill. He unloads my luggage and leads me down to a semi-rusted steel door below. The steel, he points out, has been allowed to rust naturally, then waxed so that the rust does not rub off. Inside, the room is sleek and spare, with smooth, hard surfaces in wood, marble, and glass. A wall of glass faces out over the ocean, which is fierce and unwelcoming through a veil of chill, grey mist. There is a fireplace, however, and a pile of wood, some twiggy, nouveau rustique furniture arranged around it. The bellhop gestures under the bed, where, he informs me, two massage tables are stowed. Massages can be done solo or in tandem, he says, inside or out on the deck, with or without a glass of wine.

He leaves at last, and I turn on the heat. I sit on the couch, which is as uncomfortable as it looks, to read the hotel's literature. There is a card offering tarot readings ("renewed insight into the meaning of life's journey"), a list of expensive spa treatments, yoga classes, the inevitable injunctions to stay on the path and away from the wildlife. And then, considering a tandem massage in the bracing Northern California wind, with a glass of wine, the Pacific raging below, and then a fire to come in to, the huge platform stage of a bed, Nature looking on, the terry robes in the closet and the basking pool awaiting—suddenly I realize that this place is really a setup for ecologically charged trysts. Except for the exorbitant nightly rate, the up-to-the-minute restaurant, the slick appointments, it is not much different from its hokier sixties cousin down the road. Give or take a few phrases, a few hundred thousand dollars here and there, the message is still Love. And Profit.

✱

BUMPING THROUGH THE African bush, exploring a new game reserve there, I find that reverential rot travels far and fast. "Before you think staying with us costs the earth," says the brochure, "consider that might just be what saves it."

Clever, this—despite its grammatical precariousness—the familiar sting in the tail, the smiling threat, the way the injunction plays to the twin indulgences of our age: self-righteousness and guilt. Ten thousand miles from

California and there's no getting away from it. This is a world of Reverence for Harmony and Biodiversity, for The Wilderness Ethic, and, of course, for Eco-Tourism. This is not, in fact, a game reserve, but a Resource Reserve. It is run by a consortium of Eco-Entrepreneurs, dedicated to bringing wild animals back into the region. And, of course, the wildlife tourists right behind them.

The ranger tells me that he has a degree in Lifestyle Management. The Eco-Entrepreneurs, he says, want to change the lifestyle of the local farmers and poachers, to bring them into Harmony with the Resource Reserve by providing them with employment. Animals are being brought in all the time—some from other reserves, some from wildlife auctions. If they are not apparent—in two days, we have seen nothing larger than a dung beetle—it is because the elephants and lions are "recovering from their capture experience. And your leopard and cheetah are hard to spot."

I am relieved. This ranger does not fill me with confidence. Unlike rangers I have had in other reserves—messianic devotees of the bush, many of whom grew up there and want to die there—this one is dying to go to America. When he gets there, he says, he will spend a whole week in Disneyland. Perhaps, I think, he is the new-style ranger. A city man, with a degree in Lifestyle Management.

Or perhaps the old-style ones are in short supply. Since Eco-Tourism has become such big business, the rangers themselves must double as salesmen. Not only must they understand your lion and your leopard, but they must also chat with your tourist back at the camp over tea or dinner, and look as if they like it. In contrast to Brown Shirt of California, the fault here can lie in a sort of smarmy determination to please. Like the single men hired by cruise ships to dance with the widows.

The camp itself is built on a rise, overlooking the bush. It is luxurious, casually arranged, with a pool, bungalows for the guests, and a central building housing the dining room and lounge, the office and curio shop. In the much larger, old-fashioned, state-run game reserves, the camps are surrounded by high fences to keep the animals out. Outside the camps—for the sake of the animals, and of the people, and of the bush itself—tourists must stay inside their cars, and stick to the roads. And they must be back in camp by sunset.

In these more luxurious Eco-Resource-Arrangements, however, there are no fences, and the game drives go on night and day. Tourists sit in open Land Rovers like cupcakes on a bakery tray. They stop for sundowners or even private dinners in the bush. In camp, they wander freely down to the pool and back to their bungalows, as if they were in Hawaii, the Costa Brava, Cap Ferrat. After dinner, they sit on the open verandah, listening to the sounds of the bush and to the beautiful, young, tanned rangers telling stories. They consider Life and Death, Nature, Being, Love—

And then, one evening after I leave, a guest, trotting along the path past the swimming pool, happens to be pounced on by a lioness and is eaten. When the press contacts the Eco-Entrepreneurs, they are told that this has simply been a case of mistaken identity. Upright Man, they explain, is not the natural prey of lions. Had the guest been whistling or singing as she walked along the path, she would not have seemed so un-human. On the other hand, had the lioness not lost her natural fear of Man while recovering from her capture experience, she might never have come anywhere near the camp.

∗

BACK HOME, WALKING through the cosmetic section of a large department store, I am handed a card by a smiling saleswoman, who is promoting a "fragrance." Inside the card is a perfumed ribbon, which I throw away. The card itself, however, I read. It is full of wisdom on the nature of dunes. "They play a critical ecological role," it says, "in the Earth's complex chain of life." When visiting a dune, the card tells me, do this, don't do that. I decide then and there never to visit a dune. And not any other ecologically significant site of Recreation either. If I do happen upon a dune, as I have on occasion, I shall try not to see it as having a critical ecological role in the Earth's complex chain of life. And I shall try not to make it a Humbling Experience. I shall try never to Surrender to its Empowerment. Never. Never. Never.

It's a Small, Unnatural World

I WAS THERE BECAUSE OF A PROMISE TO A CHILD. IT HAD seemed so safe, three thousand miles from California, to play Lady Bountiful, perched on the side of my nine-year-old godchild's bed, saying magnificently, "One day, Aunty will take you to Disneyland."

But now there he was, thumbs plugging away at a Game Boy while our bus edged through the Los Angeles traffic, onto the freeway, onto another freeway. He looked up and beamed at me. "I killed a flower! Did you see me kill that flower, Aunty?"

Seventeen years before, I had gone to Disneyland with my own daughter. I'd known then, had known even before I went, that the place would hold no charm for me. Perhaps, I'd thought, I lacked the necessary childhood, growing up in a country where my Snow White and Cinderella and Winnie the Pooh and Peter Pan were not Disney's. Where Minnie and Mickey and Goofy and the rest were creatures of the Saturday-afternoon cartoons at the cinema, characters I had found neither endearing nor funny.

The bus drew up outside the hotel—one in a row of chains and franchise operations on a wide and busy thoroughfare outside the park. The hotel was run by Indians, some of them from Zambia, a sort of Anaheim Masala. The desk clerk beamed at us. "Velcome to Disneyland!" he said.

The boy looked from him to me and then around the lobby. He seemed worried that this, perhaps, was it. Disneyland. He was a worried sort of boy, old-fashioned and polite. On the shuttle to the park, he'd listened carefully to the information the driver gave us. Over 250 million visitors to Disneyland since 1955, including kings and queens and princes and princesses.

Inside the park, people roamed about in groups, many wearing the local regalia—Mickey Mouse ears, Donald Duck beaked caps, crowns, capes. I asked the boy whether he'd like a set of ears himself, but he shook his head vigorously. "Where should we start, Aunty?" he asked. He was keen to get on with it, that was clear. But I wanted lunch. And I needed to examine the souvenir guidebook with map that I'd been given at the gate. I was hopeless and still am at that sort of touring. And not much good with maps. When I travel, I tend to wander, following a mood. The wandering itself, in fact, creates the mood, seems to give order to life, and hope. But, in that sort of orderly place, I felt lost and insignificant. It was the reason I had never been amused by amusement parks, not even as a child. Still, there was the boy, his dark, earnest eyes trained on me. "Are you happy with our new president, Aunty?" he said.

We settled into the corner of what looked like an ice cream parlor for lunch. The boy was given crayons and a placemat with puzzles and a maze. I studied the map. The park seemed vast, with huge distances to cover between Main Street and anywhere. Not so far, the waitress assured me, delivering a hamburger and a peanut butter and jelly sandwich with a heap of corn chips in the shape of Mickey Mouse heads. It's an easy walk, she said. She did it every day.

She was right, of course. Although the map seemed fashioned to resemble the Congo Basin, the park, I realized, was quite contained. It was arranged like a miniature empire, with countries to visit in space and time—Frontierland, Tomorrowland, Fantasyland, Adventureland. Had I not been with a child, I would have found it excruciating to have to ask the way to such places. Like asking for a lipstick called Hot Stuff or Moist Tomato.

After lunch, we made our way to Dumbo the Flying Elephant in less than ten minutes and found a line just long enough to have the boy trembling with desire to be airborne.

In front of us, a girl in mouse ears wailed, "I wanna go on the pink one! I wanna go on the pink one!"

"Shuddup!" the mother snapped. "You hafta go on the one they tell ya!"

My boy was ecstatic with the ride. Round and round we went, up and down. "Can we go again, Aunty?" he asked, when we landed. And so we joined the back of the line again, snaking our way up to the front.

Next we found It's a Small World. Somehow, over all the years, the theme song of this ride has lived on, like Mr. Rogers's "Beautiful Day" and the opening theme to *Sesame Street*. And then, sure enough, there it was, the chipmunk chorus, chirping its paean to the oneness of humankind as we sailed past identical Mattel dolls smiling and dancing in their grass skirts and yashmaks, their pareos and dirndls, their dark skin and light skin. "It's a world of laughter, a world of tears."

The boy was enchanted. Back in the daylight, climbing out of the boat, he turned to me and said, "I'm so happy in this place, Aunty." I grabbed him up and kissed him, which he endured with fortitude. People waiting in the line opposite smiled at us. But what I wanted to tell this serious, sweet child was that I wished him quite a different sort of happiness. Something grounded in a real place—a place without an idea behind it. Somewhere fertile and mysterious, ancient and beautiful.

That night, he suffered an acute attack of homesickness. For this, I knew, there was no real cure. And so I told him stories of my own homesickness—how I'd carried on as a child, and as an adult too. He smiled a bit at this, the idea of an adult crying, and then he fell asleep. The next morning, before sunrise, he was awake, cured, and at the Game Boy again. "I'm running out of time," he mumbled, punching furiously. "If I get the star, I'll be invincible."

Back at the park, he took over the guidebook. We started with the shops, where he chose a Donald Duck from me, gifts to take home, and a pennant for himself. I suggested that we come back to buy them on the way out. "Do you think you should write that down, Aunty?" he suggested politely.

Sitting through the Jungle Cruise, I realized that the park seemed a little worn since last I'd been here. And that the old rides themselves were dated. Even the water was murky and smelled like an old, still pond. In a way, the shabbiness lent a sort of wacky amusement to the experience after all. The newer rides were wilder, more terrifying, with a deadly seriousness to them. But these old plastic crocodiles and hippopotamuses, the black bearers in khaki and red fezzes being driven up a tree by a rhinoceros, the worn-out patter of the guide on our boat in his safari togs and hat—well, this was just the old Disney-eye view of the world. Miles from ecological, political, environmental, and nutritional correctitude. It didn't seem nearly as sad as the tourists videoing a large male gorilla with red glass eyes beating his chest in a fury.

With time running out, we decided on the Submarine Voyage, where we were launched on another journey through a large, smelly pond, this time underwater. To the strains of a sea shanty, we floated past plastic fish and giant clams, buried treasure and bits of sea monster. Over the loudspeaker came a rich baritone talking of the taming of the restless sea and our last frontier on the planet earth.

"I thought there were going to be real things down there," the boy said as we climbed out, showing his first sign of impatience. He wished now we'd had another go at the Rocket Jets instead. He was even pouting.

"Nothing is real in Disneyland, darling," I assured him, trying to take his hand.

But he sighed and plunged his hands into his pockets. "Except the people," he said, heading back toward the shops.

The Beach of the Lost World

THE GREAT HORROR OF MY ADOLESCENCE, A TIME SPENT in the subtropical sun, was not skin cancer but pregnancy. To have one's life circumscribed by shameful and premature motherhood spelled, for girls like me—virgins in bathing suits, swanning along the beach in gorgeous tans and sophisticated sunglasses—a sort of early death.

And so the closest we could come to being naked in front of a man was to wear a bikini. Bikinis had been around in Europe for twenty years, but in South Africa they only came into the light in the early sixties. There we were, girls in our new bikinis, plunging into the sea under the eyes of men, and then emerging from the water, hair streaming, salt stinging, to stretch out in the sun without conscience.

Day after day the sun shone, friend to all but the whitest-skinned among us. They were pitied like the sick, huddled as they were under hats and umbrellas. For the rest of us, oiling our skins in the sun like fine leather, working for the flawless cappuccino tan that was the ne plus ultra of real beauty in that world, there was no more thought given to wrinkles, mottles, or lesions than to Medicare and assisted living. In fact, we lived in happy ignorance of anything but good from the sun, children that we were of the Southern Hemisphere with its glorious beaches and endless summers.

Those were the lovely years for me, sprung at last from my girls' school and pretending to be in control of my life. In fact, I was only in control of the few men whom I had managed to enthrall. Until that point, and for all the years of my adolescence, I would go down to the beach every Sunday morning as to a school in its own right. In the large Indian Ocean port in which I grew up, the beach itself was the chief proving ground of a girl's future. There, clustered around the wall—Jews on North Beach, Gentiles on South Beach—she would practice for a husband, trying to distinguish herself among the writhing mass of semi-naked, semi-chaste youth, all of them jousting, feinting, preening, until they were old enough to pair off formally and announce their engagements in the newspaper.

Watching those pairs, I was nothing but wary for my own future. To be nailed through the foot before you'd even had a chance at the real world. To be caught, still lithe and tanned and oiled, so that in a year or so you'd be sitting under an umbrella, first one baby and then one or two more, a nanny tucking up her skirt to wade into the surf with a bucket. Well, this was almost as much of a horror to me as the unmarried mothers' home itself.

What I wanted for myself, what I had dreamed of all through childhood, was a future far away, in what I had always thought of as the real world. Ideally, it would include basking on yachts in the Mediterranean, dining alfresco in strapless evening gowns. Ours was a society that had always looked north for glamour, mostly to Europe, and often in terms of the films we'd seen, the photographs in magazines.

And so, when my first shot north arrived with an invitation to spend a year in America as a foreign exchange student, it seemed perfectly normal to have my mother outfitting me as if for a grand European tour. How were any of us to know that I was plunging into a world of wraparound skirts, Peter Pan collars, penny loafers, and Bermuda shorts? How could we have imagined that an eighteen-year-old virgin, accustomed to a world in which older men took her dinner-dancing at night clubs, would feel as brazen there as a streetwalker in her high heels and backless frocks?

Home again after the year, back on the beach and out of clothes at last, I found I had graduated from the wall to the sand. I was newly thin, having lost the weight I had gained in America, and a few extra pounds as well. Let no one say that losing weight does not change one's life. It does; it has. For the first time since childhood I was in possession of my body in a way that did not require special breathing.

Meanwhile, I began to collect men on the beach, careful to fall in love with the one I would be least likely to marry. I bought myself an old Morris Minor and drove here, there, down to the beach whenever I liked, drunk on my newfound independence.

When my best friend married and built herself a house up the coast, she found herself beset by marauding bands of monkeys, and the surrounding bush infested with deadly black mambas. Even the beach was useless: without shark nets, no one but a fool would have swum in the sea. And so she moved back into town. Before she'd married, we'd often spent the afternoons at her pool once the wind picked up on the beachfront. It was a lovely pool, set high in the garden, with lawns rolling downhill, and a view of the sea. Often there'd be others, too. And tea would be served. We played host and guest, with little of the swagger and throb, the vast roiling theatre of the beach to the game.

My unmarriageable lover scorned these afternoons. It was the beach he loved, windy or not. Sometimes, in the late afternoons, when the families and vendors were gone, we would walk to the end of the pier to see what the Indian fishermen had caught. If the surf was calm, we might swim out as far as the shark nets, coming back in, wave after wave, to lie on the sand and catch the last long rays of the sun. And already I'd be homesick for what I hadn't yet left behind.

"There's madness in his family," my mother would warn me when I came home. She understood quite well the romance of the beach. When she and my father fell defiantly in love, he would take her down there at night with a picnic basket and a bottle of champagne. So how could I expect her to believe that, for me, defiance was one thing, marriage quite another? How could I admit to anyone how alarmed I was becoming myself at the approach of a time when I would be finished at university and marooned down there at the bottom of the world?

Meanwhile, there were long walks along the surf, spontaneous excursions up the coast for oysters and crayfish. Sometimes, when it was hot and still, we'd go swimming at night, the sea still warm and black as ink. People said it was dangerous, and probably they were right. But, floating out on the swells, invisible, with the sound of the surf and the lights of the city across the water, it seemed like an idyll out of time and place.

And then, one day, I was stopped by the sight of a newcomer. He was pale and freckled, nothing like the tanned, muscled habitués of our world. He had stretched himself out on a deck chair some way off and was reading Kafka's *Amerika*. I still don't know why the sight of him provoked me as it did. People were always bringing books down to the beach, often to show off. But this man's showing off had a sneer to it, a sort of challenge. I had to go right up to him and stand between him and the sun before he would even lower his book and look at me.

That evening he drove me up the coast in his Alfa Romeo, ninety miles per hour on the wrong side of the road. As we hurtled through the darkness, he talked quite easily. He was leaving for America in a few weeks, he said, he had only come down to the coast to say goodbye to his parents. Would he miss them, I asked? Would he miss all this? Oh no, he said, sweeping me easily around the dance floor, he already had tickets for next year's season at the Boston Symphony, a whole life there to look forward to.

A small scholarship carried me to Boston, marriage to the reader of Kafka, and five years of graduate school in New York. For the months before I had left, my unmarriageable lover had tried to stop me from going. He took me by the shoulders and stared fiercely into my face, asking again and again if I knew how ordinary my life would be in such a world, how tethered, how loveless, how cold and unworthy.

But the future had taken hold of me with an equally fierce grip, and I couldn't give it up. And even though I knew he was right—even though I knew there'd be nothing again like the glorious world I was leaving behind—still I kept telling myself, the plane lifting from the runway, that it could never have lasted anyway.

Honky, Napoleon, and the Empress Wu

THE DOG WAS MY FAULT. I KNEW PERFECTLY WELL THAT a Pekinese would be wrong in a household of Ridgebacks and Irish setters. I also knew that one didn't buy puppies from a pet shop. Our dogs came in as rogues—the runt of someone's litter, or a stray, or a gun-shy hunter that refused to breed. But, at thirteen, severely discontented with the dos and don'ts of life, I wanted to see just how far the determination to do the wrong thing might take me. And so I nagged.

Even after the heart was out of my petition, I kept it up. As the youngest child in a large establishment of family and servants, I seldom had my way with anything. And so meal after meal I harangued them. I just did not know how to stop.

But then, one day, quite suddenly and to my alarm, my parents gave in. *Enough!* they said. They were *sick* of me! Sick of the sound of my *voice*! *Okay!* they said, the *bloody* puppy! *Fine!*

So, there he was now—a nervous little creature scuttling under a chair if anyone, person or dog, approached him. He yapped and squealed and wet the carpet, and if someone reached down for him, he bit. After a while he bit even if you didn't reach down for him, darting up to nip an ankle or a foot. And he was particularly fond of biting children.

"If one weren't a bit squeamish," my mother said, "one would simply tell one of the servants to drown it." She was sitting across the couch from my father, well into her first glass of Scotch.

He ran a hand across his brow, which was to say he'd had a long day and this sort of thing was not what he wished to come home to.

"If anyone drowns him," I shouted, "I'll report you the SPCA!" I was rolling around on the floor with the big dogs, not much caring what was decided, although I still felt obliged to keep up my side of things.

My father slammed down his glass. Reporting anyone for anything was not the way we did things. And it *wasn't* funny. He was about to bellow something to this effect when Emma arrived in the doorway.

"Master," she said, "I knock, but no one they hear me."

"Yes, Emma?"

"The small dog he can stay with me." She closed her lips over her enormous front teeth and cupped her hands, one into the other, in formal supplication.

This was startling, not because she had overheard our conversation—news in that house, despite its large rooms and thick walls, seemed to carry, as if by magic, to wherever the servants happened to be—but because Africans generally did not like dogs, and for good reason. Just let an African walk past a house, and the dogs would be after him, roaring, snarling, leaping at the fence. Let him set foot inside the gate, and he'd need a stick or a whip to defend himself.

The improbable thing was that Emma had fallen in love with this puppy from the start. Perhaps, for her, as for our other dogs, he wasn't really a dog at all. Whenever the dogs saw him, they would rush up in a pack as if chasing a cat. And then she, who, as part of the household was exempt from their terrorizing, would come bustling in, shooing them off, heaving her large bulk onto her knees so that she could coax him out from under the chair with a few lines of "Sentimental Journey."

Song was as natural to Emma as talking. More natural, in a way. Out in the laundry, she sang the hymns she'd grown up with—"Rock of Ages," "The Lord's My Shepherd." If I happened to walk past, she'd gesture madly for me to join in, so that she could harmonize. She could harmonize with any hymn, any song, even those she didn't know.

She had grown up in a Methodist mission station in Zululand, the daughter of a Methodist preacher. As a teenager, she'd been sent to the city, like other Zulu girls, to go into domestic service. How difficult this had been for her—how much homesickness played in the hymn-singing out there—I never asked myself. I just sang along, teaching her some of the hymns we sang in prayers at my Christian school, and a song or two I'd learned in my afternoon Hebrew classes. Soon I'd hear her trying them out, adding ornaments here and there, turning minor to major to cheer things up a bit as she wielded the iron, serenading the puppy.

And the strange thing was that he never bit her. When he heard her voice, he'd push his flat little snout out from wherever he was hiding, and then wriggle out into the open, wagging, licking, trying to clamber into her lap. Soon, he was trotting happily after her in the house like a small mobile mop. If the other dogs became too much of a nuisance, she would scoop him up and put him into the pocket of her apron, singing to calm him down.

She had learned popular songs from the kitchen radio, which she would plug and unplug as she moved from room to room, dusting, tidying, making the beds. She listened not only to the hit parade, but also to the morning soap operas, in which my parents, who were actors, often played parts. If the story was becoming too tense to bear, she would come shyly, like now, at drinks time, when she knew, as did we all, that my parents were at their mellowest, to ask them whether this character or that was, indeed, going to die, or leave her husband, and was the baby going to be a girl or a boy? She herself was hoping for a boy.

But now here she was, standing solemnly before my parents, pleading formally for the puppy's life. We had all seen her singing to him as she carried him about over the weeks. It was an eccentric situation, unprecedented for us, and everyone found it funny. Still, it had occurred to no one that she could be the solution to the problem.

My parents looked at each other as if to say, Why not? They asked her a few questions, pretended to consider. And then, nodding graciously, they pronounced her the new keeper of the dog. It was to sleep in her room in the servants' quarters. And, yes, she could name him anything she wished.

As it turned out, she had the name ready: Hong Kong, because he looked Chinese, Honky for short. No one considered this odd. *Honky* was not a word in use in South Africa then, and is not now either—not as a racial slur, nor as anything else. Anyway, none of us had ever seen a Chinese person. Under apartheid, Chinese were categorized as black; Japanese as white (although none of us had seen a Japanese person either). We'd seen photographs and films and cartoons, and so Honky was Honky, and that was that.

It was only twenty years later, once I was living in America, that I found there was another meaning to the word. I was being asked by the bank, whom I had phoned to set up an account, to choose an answer to a security question. I could choose one of various questions, all of them relating to childhood: a favorite pet? a best friend? the name of the street on which I'd lived? I chose favorite pet, and because he was the least favorite, thought I might find it easiest to remember Honky. "Honky," I said.

There was a pause. "Could you repeat that?" said the operator.

"Honky," I said again. "H-O-N-K-Y." I was used to this. My accent seemed to make me particularly difficult to understand on the telephone.

"Hold, please," she said.

I held. And held. Until, after about ten minutes, I hung up and, in some annoyance, phoned again.

This time, I was passed directly to a supervisor, someone of a different order of understanding. "All we need,"

she said curtly, "is your mother's maiden name and date
of birth. Thank you," she said, "the account is now active."

✱

HAVING A DOG in her room made difficulties for Emma
with the men of her life. When she adopted Honky, Reuben,
the houseboy, a dark, proud Congolese man, who was her
lover, ordered her to put him out of her room at night. But
Honky was not negotiable, and there were loud rows in the
servants' quarters. After some weeks or a month of this,
and quite suddenly, the authorities deported Reuben back
to the Congo, and Emma became unsmiling and doleful,
singing solemn Easter hymns as she moved through the
days, Honky in her apron pocket. I couldn't even tempt her
with "Stormy Weather," one of her favorites. "Ai, no, Bum,"
she would say, "too much work to do."

Ours was a family of nicknames. To Emma I was
Bum, another word unrelated to its American meaning. I
never asked why. To me she was Amazinyo Kanogwanga,
Rabbit Teeth, or Empress Wu of the Feathered Dog. My
first boyfriend, a plump, devoted, hapless boy, she named
Pullman Bus, Pullman for short. Bum, she'd say, Pullman
at the gate. And when, eventually, she took up with a new
man herself, someone as cross and unpleasing as she was

cheerful and pleasant, she called him Old Man, although he was no older than she was.

When I asked her to write out the words of "Nkosi Sikel' iAfrica," a hymn she and I had sung many times together, she said she would ask the Old Man to do it, he was educated and knew how to spell. But, when she asked him, he just clicked his tongue. "Ai, suka!" he said. Old Man was political, she whispered to me, he was educated. By which I took it that he was annoyed by the idea of a white girl presuming to learn a black hymn.

Emma herself, who had had to leave school after Standard Four, was a keen reader. Every night she read *Napoleon's Book of Fate* to find out what lay ahead. She also read the Bible, and the newspaper, and taught herself to read recipes and to calculate times and temperatures when she had to take over as cook. But she was not political. Political in the fifties and sixties was a dangerous thing to be, and for Emma it held no romance at all.

Her romance lay in the songs she sang. "Sentimental Journey," "Now Is The Hour," "Tennessee Waltz." There was also the holy romance of praise and supplication— "Jesu, lover of my soul," "O God, Our Help in Ages Past." She sang to console herself, or to lift her heart, to rejoice if there was something to rejoice over, or just to keep herself and Honky company when there was no one around to join in.

In a household of mild eccentrics, she fit in quite nicely. Every now and then, for instance, she was in the habit of hauling one of her enormous breasts out of her uniform and leaving it hanging there like a balloon. This she did with such pride and good humor that it seemed to me simply something she did, the way my father wrapped his head in a silk scarf every morning, like a pirate, to straighten out his curls. Anyway, it was often perishingly hot in our subtropical climate, and she was a large woman, who wore thick stockings for her varicose veins, and wool slippers with pom-poms for her flat feet. So perhaps she was just cooling off.

Whatever the case, I'd laugh along, and, when I was still a child and she supervising my bath, reach out for the baby powder and shower the breast with it to turn it white. "You naught!" she would say, happily brushing the powder off. And then on we'd go with my bath, she reminding me yet again to save up some urine to wash my face, it was good for the skin.

"Bum," she wrote, once I had left home and was living in America, "Wu finish with the old man. My mind is made up. I am too old to wait so I have come to the conclusion that I walk to you in America if you do not send for me. Honky he give away. Time for me to leave."

Honky given away? I wrote to my parents, remonstrating loudly. But my mother just wrote back to say that, when they'd moved from the big house to a smaller maisonette, they could take only one dog with them, and that was, of course, Simba, the last of the Ridgebacks. They'd found an elderly teacher, however, long retired, who was only too pleased to have Honky, although she'd changed his name to Fluff.

"Dearest Child," Emma wrote, "surprise for you. Wu is got no teeth all gone. Please let me know about the life there in America. I am get old and I like to know everything. Who sing with you now? Who laugh?"

No one was the answer. I was married to a sour, humorless man, who happened also to be tone deaf. "Oh, Amazinyo Kanogwanga," I wrote back, "I'm coming home in July!"

She was waiting in the driveway as we drove in from the airport. There she stood without her teeth, her whole face sunken in, her body, too, it seemed. "Oh, Em-Bem!" I cried, "no more Amazinyo Kanogwanga!"

She laughed, all gums, and Nicholas, the new house-boy, laughed behind her, carrying in my suitcases. "Wu she get old, Bum," she lisped, "too late now for America. You must come home."

The next time I came home, she was dying. When I went to see her at McCord Zulu Hospital, she looked up out of the skeleton that was left of her. "Bum," she whispered, "please bring *Napoleon's Book of Fate*. Please bring XXX Mints."

But when I came with the book and the mints the next day, her bed was stripped and empty. The patient in the next bed closed her eyes and turned her face to the wall.

I stood where I was, holding the worn old book, as awkward as if I were being asked to believe a lie. A photograph was closed into it, keeping a place. Emma and Honky under the mango tree, I had taken it myself. She had composed herself for the camera, Honky under one arm, her lips closed solemnly over the enormous teeth.

Soon her family would be coming to claim what she had left behind, people I hardly knew. They'd knock at the kitchen door, asking for my father, wanting money for the funeral—a goat or a pig.

I tucked the photograph into my pocket and made my way out of the hospital. Nicholas would be making fried sole and chips for lunch today. When Emma began to feel ill, my mother had instructed her to teach him how to cook. But she had just turned her back so that he couldn't see what she was doing, and my mother, who couldn't cook herself, had had to intervene.

I stood out in the sunshine, breathing in the heat of the day. In a few weeks I'd be returning to America. For the rest of my life, I thought, I'd be arriving and returning like this, everything loosening and shifting over time, with less to leave behind me, another world to come home to again.

Inheriting the Past

FOR DECADES AFTER LEAVING SOUTH AFRICA, HOME was in two places: America, where I lived, and South Africa, to which I went home. Home there, as arranged by my parents before I was born, seemed gloriously fixed with its serious furniture, serious paintings, silver, crystal, the tea tray clinking down the passage and the E-flat of the dinner gong. There was something abiding in it that gave a sort of pick-up-and-go lightness to the series of accommodations I'd lived in on both coasts of the U.S., landing up in a charming Victorian bungalow in California, looking out over acres of vineyards.

And then my father died and the equation failed. The old house was broken up, many of its contents shipped to me in America by my oldest sister, who had serious arrangements of her own. I had chosen them days before leaving

South Africa, and in a miasma of disbelief. Even as I listed couch and chairs, two suites of crystal, tea sets, a tea service, it seemed impossible that I could claim them at all, that they could sail across to my other life and fit in there. And yet, if I didn't claim them, my oldest sister assured me, they would be auctioned off to strangers, and, in any case, there would still be nothing left to come home to.

For the next nine months, while the things were packed into crates and then a container, shipped across the Atlantic, unloaded in Baltimore and then trucked across the country, I worried obsessively about how I would deploy them when they arrived, where they would fit. I had taken photographs and measurements of the furniture before I left, but now, back in my own house, I was beset by doubts about how they would translate—that world with its spacious rooms, high ceilings, deep verandahs, into this.

My living and dining rooms were already a bazaar of overstuffed furniture, Oriental rugs, Oriental pillows, old photographs and antique maps on the walls, bookshelves everywhere, and a looming grand piano in the bay window.

I've never been much good at imagining the way things will look before actually seeing them in place. And so, over the years, I've become an old hand at furniture moving. But then, with only measurements and photographs in hand, I could imagine nothing. I had to take it on faith that the

Georgian grandfather clock would enhance any room it inhabited, that my parents' large deco couch and chairs— formal, well designed, solidly made—would improve on my own overstuffed set in a William Morris fabric.

The real problem, I thought, would lie with the massive old Zanzibar chest. It was meant for large spaces, much larger than anything I could provide. And yet it was that chest I most desperately wanted to find a place for. I loved it; I had always loved it standing there in the huge hall at home, with its enormous brasses, its giant key, and, on top, the miniature galleon, brass bowls, claw-footed boxes, and mortar and pestle.

On the day the furniture was to be delivered, I felt as I feel every time I take a trip—that I desperately wanted to turn back. For all the comparative lightness of my life, I had found, lately, that I was feeling weighted down by things— their acquisition, their upkeep, their security. For some time, I had been dreaming obsessively of ways to free myself from them. And now here, any minute, would be the truck drawing up outside the house, loaded down with more.

*

FIRST OUT WAS the grandfather clock. My parents had loved that clock with its ornate crown and face, "Tempus

Fugit" on a plaque above the dial, its dings and rolling chimes. It was by far the most valuable piece of furniture they owned, the sort of piece that stays in families for generations. Both sisters had decided that I should have it, and even though I had never cared much for grandfather clocks, even this one, it had seemed blasphemous to refuse. And so now here it was, dwarfing the living room despite the ten-foot ceilings. I would have to move it to the hall, call in an expert to set up the weights and pulleys, and then try to sleep through the rolling chimes.

Next came the couch and chairs, lurching absurdly up the steps. I pointed to the fireplace—the couch on one side, the chairs on the other—and then, once they were in place, stood back to have a look. They stared solemnly at each other like grim old aunts, with the clock laughing down on the whole scene from the opposite wall. I edged them this way, that way, the movers lolling up against the doorway. "Looks good," they said, "Looks fine to me."

I shook my head. They didn't look fine. They were too solid, too enormous, too formal for my living room. They needed more space around them, chrome and glass, and different pictures on the wall. Panicked, I dashed off to phone a designer friend for advice. "Just try living with them for a while," she said, "and then decide." But I couldn't bear to live with them another minute. They seemed full of blame for the journey they had had to make, that life to this, the cost of the journey as well. I sent them out to the garage and had my old set brought back in.

Small tables, paintings, rugs, boxes of china and silver, boxes of old photographs and linen—these came next. And then, at last, the Zanzibar chest, both movers bent under the load of it. Before they could set it down, I stuck a Teflon furniture glide under each corner, got out of the way as they lowered it to the floor. There it was in the middle of my house, ripped from its moorings, like the object of a theft.

Still, still, I thought, I would make it more my own willy-nilly. With the help of the glides, I pushed it up against one wall of the dining room, and then against another. Wrong, all wrong. And then, in desperation, I pushed it into the living room, behind the couch, and the couch closer to the fireplace. When I'd laid the newspaper pattern there, it had seemed impossibly big for the space. But now, backing away to have a look, I saw that it was perfect, more perfect than anything else in the house—that it might always have been there, that relic of a colonial era long before my time.

I found the key strapped to the handle at the side, turned it in the lock, and lifted the enormous lid to see what was inside. It was packed with old letters—my grandparents', my father's, my mother's, mine to them— eiderdowns, pillows, linen sheets. I breathed them in, and, with them, the smell of home—cigars, spiced wood, camphor, damp, and the salt air.

I closed the lid and ran for the huge basket of ostrich eggs on top of the piano, put it on the chest. The whole arrangement looked right, so right that it began to make sense, even for a moment, of the enterprise.

*

ONCE THE MOVERS had left, I set about unpacking the boxes in the kitchen. Out came platters and dishes, tea sets, coffee sets, crystal, cut glass bowls, a suite of deco silver, a horn-handled carving set, a dozen pink glass ashtrays I hadn't seen for years, silver trays, more ashtrays, a majolica vase, a gorgeous basalt blue glass lamp. I had to stop for breath. I was unpacking my life—the theatre parties and vast family dinners, Sunday lunch, my mother's passion for style in every cup and saucer.

I filled the kitchen sink with soapy water. The dishes were dusty, some quite stained. I washed them in relays—china first, then silver—dried them, stacked them on the counters. I boiled a kettle of water and laid a tray for tea with the linen tray cloth, the small silver teapot, a cup and saucer from the old celadon tea set, a plate of shortbread, and I carried it out to the living room.

There, with the sun setting over the vineyards, the familiar heft of the teapot, the sight of the cup in my hand, the spoon on the saucer, my life suddenly seemed lightened, somehow, with these things back in it. And if I longed for the old life to live again—home here, home there, the distance between them—well, from now on, I knew, this would be as close as I could come to it.

A Stranger in My House

WHEN I HIRED MY FIRST CLEANING WOMAN IN AMERICA, it never occurred to me that I would have any difficulty with the role of employer. I had grown up, after all, in a servant society, albeit one of the most notorious. In South Africa, we had had five servants, four of them living on the premises, and although I had never seen my mother cook or clean, or even tidy up, I had grown up watching her give orders. I had also suffered the misery of her upbraiding the servants, threatening them, firing them. Her vaunted ability "to keep a servant" seemed, somehow, connected to the quality of her discontent. And so, when I left home and came to America, it was a relief to have to clean and cook for myself.

I soon noticed, however, that mention of servants in America would stop a conversation dead. The word *servant* itself, unadorned by euphemism, was shocking. It seemed to bring to mind not *service* but *servility* and *servitude*, *slavery* in fact. It also seemed to carry with it a boast of privilege for the served. Americans, I found, do not like to be "served," they like to be "helped." And, even though *Upstairs, Downstairs* and then *Downton Abbey* might bring the country to a standstill every Sunday night, the fairy tale here—played out in the kitchens and classrooms of America—was that everyone was as good as everyone else.

And then into my life came Purificación. She had emigrated from Manila about a year before and was living with her husband and three children in one room in a dingy part of town. This much I knew from the friend who had recommended her as a cleaning woman. "Just make a list," my friend advised me, "show her where everything is, and leave."

But I could not just leave a strange woman in my house. Anyway, I wanted to point things out, things that I particularly wanted done. The list was a good idea, I thought. It took the edge off the awkwardness I felt in giving orders. In America there seemed to be no leads on how to cope with the difference in our circumstances, Purificación's and mine. American friends, whose own parents had been quite comfortable hiring help, were as bad at this as I was. And now our children, grown up, seem to be continuing the charade. It is as if each generation comes upon the idea of hiring "help" de novo, everyone conspiring to regard it as a temporary arrangement. For all but academic purposes, the word *class* has joined *servant* as unutterable. In a perfect classless society, the unstated credo goes, there would be no need of servants, no need to serve.

And so, at eight o'clock one Friday morning, when I opened the door to a diminutive woman, about fifteen years older than I, I was, quite naturally, without a text. I stood back as she took off her street shoes and parked them at the door. I offered to take her coat, offered her a cup of tea, which she accepted, sitting without invitation at the dining room table, her bare feet folded under the chair. I sat there too, rolling automatically into the sort of self-mocking, chummy patter with which I am afflicted in awkward situations. "Call me Puri," she said after a while. "Everyone they call me Puri."

When tea was over, I led Puri on a tour of the house, the list still folded in my pocket. There was no question, of course, of trying out my mother's tone and posture. But I could not even bring myself to tell her straight that I did not want her to use Ajax on the bathtub. It was as if she were a guest in my house, my husband's aunt, perhaps. Someone not predisposed to look kindly on me.

I retreated to my study and stayed there all morning, listening to the broom, the vacuum, the water running.

Once, I picked up the phone and she was on it. And then I thought I heard the hair dryer and crept out into the hall to listen. As midday approached, I began to wonder about lunch. How would I do it without including her? The question carried implications not only for that Friday, but for all the future Fridays Puri would be coming to my house. And then, just as I had decided to make two sandwiches and take mine back to my study, there she was in the kitchen doorway, and I was asking her warmly to join me.

To my surprise, it soon became clear that, in the matter of employer-employee behavior, Puri was as clueless as I was. It was I, not she, in fact, who was more like an aunt. That day at lunch, she began to ask me advice in her halting, guttural English—a school for her daughter, a job for her husband. As the weeks and months passed, she consulted me on every subject imaginable—health, sex, circumcision, marriage, taxes, the floods of relatives that kept coming in to live with her. She was fascinated, too, by the cost of things—a new set of sheets I had bought, a new coat. She asked what I earned, how much I paid in rent. It was clear that she was bent on getting her family out of their one room and into the American mainstream. And I, old immigrant to new, dispensed advice, laxatives, aspirin, old clothes, recipes, the names of my doctors and my dentist.

By the time a few years had passed, Puri's family had indeed moved into a flat, and then bought a house, televisions, a Pontiac GTO. And I had learned how to bring the chats to a close when I wanted to. I had also learned that using the subjunctive made it easier to ask her to do things: "Would you mind—?" "Could you, when you have the time—?" I had even begun to leave the house when she was there. And if I came back to find her on the telephone, or sitting at my dressing table, applying my blush and eye shadow, I learned to show my displeasure by turning away in silence. And then I grumbled privately about her to my friends. Still, I never did find a way of letting her know she was not invited to join in the conversation when friends came over for tea. Nor did I know how to stem the flood of invitations that she issued to her graduations, confirmations, baptisms, and then, one day, to her Silver Wedding.

There was no question of not going to the Silver Wedding. Puri had been consulting me for months about hiring a hall, the wedding cake she wanted decorated in silver, whether to use paper plates or what? Anyway, I could not bear to have her think I might not want to go. It was as if all her years in America had been tending toward this and I had a stake in the journey.

When I arrived, she threw her arms around me, took me over to meet an auntie, a cousin, pointed out the table at which I was to sit. Others were seated there already, about six or seven sober-looking Caucasian Americans. The rest of the guests were Filipino, happily greeting each other, waving, hugging, laughing.

I made my way to the table and sat down. We all smiled politely at each other. Someone mentioned Puri's gown, someone else her new house. A man asked where I came from, and I told him. Then the conversation fell flat. Until Puri rushed across the dance floor with a platter of egg rolls. "Doctor he is my Tuesday!" she announced. "Patty she works for Federal Reserve Bank! She is my Monday! You and Patty, you both got dogs!" She laughed merrily, called one of her sons over to pour us more sparkling wine, and then took off again.

Sitting there, my head beginning to swim from the heat and the wine, I smiled at the thought of trying to explain this event to my mother. Trying to explain America itself.

Viva Mandela!

I'VE BEEN COMING HOME LIKE THIS FOR MORE THAN twenty years—staring out of the plane window at the Valley of a Thousand Hills, the factories, the bluff, the bay, the Indian Ocean—with my heart in my throat for the familiarity of it all. This time I'm back for my father's eightieth birthday, which happens to coincide with Nelson Mandela's release from Robben Island. And I have a brief to write about the reaction of the local Africans.

I step out of the plane and into the dense heat of a Durban summer day. Next to me in the passport line is an Indian holding a South African passport. He's wearing a white crocheted skullcap, white slacks, white sandals, and a white T-shirt with "CALVIN KLEIN" printed across the front.

"What a day to arrive," I say.

He gives me a wary look. "Hot, very hot," he says, fanning himself with his passport.

On the way into town, my parents talk about who is coming to the party that night, who can't wait to see me. I ask about Mandela. Yes, they say, isn't it amazing? They have kept the morning paper in case I want to take it back with me to America.

At home, the servants are waiting for us in the driveway.

"Hello, sister," says Nicholas, the cook and general factotum. He clasps my hand and leads me into the three-way handshake of African brotherhood. I wonder whether there's new meaning to all of this today.

After I've unpacked, I wander into the kitchen to hand out presents. "What do you think about Mandela and the ANC?" I ask Nicholas.

He continues chopping onions. Fifty people are coming to the party. The cooking has been going on for days. "Some cup of tea?" he asks. "Some biscuit?"

I know that this is Buthelezi country, Zulu country, that Mandela is a Xhosa, and that there's a war of allegiance raging in the Zulu townships. But still, I can't quite believe Nicholas, Zulu or no, isn't glad about the changes. At 3 p.m. Mandela is to be set free. The event will be broadcast live. "Want to watch Mandela on television?" I ask.

He smiles at me, bearing a sparse set of rotting teeth. "Mandela!" he cries, shaking his head. "Big, big trouble!"

Regina, the maid, peeps around the laundry door to see what's going on. So does Gladys, my sister's housekeeper, who has come over to help.

"What about Mandela?" I ask them. "Is it a good thing?"

Gladys clicks her tongue. She doesn't live in servants' quarters like the others, but comes in to work every day from the township. She can read and she can drive. "People are burning down their houses," she says. "Inkatha and UDF have been at it for quite a while. I just wish they'd stuff off and get on with things!"

"É-hé!" Regina agrees. "Xhosa always think they better than everyone else! I don't like Mandela or the CNA [Central News Agency, a chain of bookstores]."

My mother wanders in to order tea. "I wouldn't stir them up, if I were you, darling," she says, leading me away to the study. "They've got their hands full with the party. And, anyway, what do they know about Mandalay?"

At the party that night, I run into a cousin whom I haven't seen for years. After ten years in Dallas, she and her husband have come back to live in Johannesburg. She wears Joan Collins makeup and a Rolex watch. We stand together in the buffet line, catching up. Isn't it amazing, I say, about Mandela?

Just that afternoon, she said, driving to the airport in Johannesburg, she found herself caught in the path of hundreds of thousands of ecstatic Africans raising their fists in the air and shouting, "Viva Mandela!" This is it, she thought, I'm dead. But then, as she edged forward through the crowd, she found herself caught up in the excitement. She lowered her window and thrust her own fist into the air. "VIVA!" she screamed. "VIVA!" A black woman in a pink maid's uniform and bare feet stopped and smiled. "Viva, Madam!" she said.

After ten days in Durban, I decide to go to the bush to see some animals. The first day out, I ask the ranger what his African spotter thinks of the turn of events. The spotter sits on a special platform at the back of the Land Rover, scanning the horizon for game. He is Shangaan and speaks only Shangaan. In this camp, spotters are not allowed to speak English.

The ranger gives me the look of a man paid to answer stupid questions. He's used to hearing them from Americans and Europeans and South Americans. I have clearly been classified as a particularly stupid South African.

"He hasn't a clue about Mandela or the ANC," he informs me quietly. "None of them has. They're much more interested in who's bewitching whom."

At the next camp, I try again. This time I ask Enoch,

a black ranger, who is unsnapping his rifle from the dashboard of his Land Rover. What does he think of the turn of events? I ask. He seems delighted by my question. "Let the ANC come here!" he cries, leveling his rifle at the road. "I'll shoot them myself!"

That evening, at sunset, several Land Rovers converge to watch two elephants playing in a dry riverbed. My Land Rover is full of minor English aristocrats. Enoch, who speaks fluent Portuguese, is next to us with a group of Brazilians. They laugh and talk so loudly that, after a while, one of the elephants turns to look. He flaps out his ears and holds them there, lifting his trunk into the air.

"I say," says Lady Muck-on-Toast behind me, "is everything all right?"

"Fine," says the ranger. But he unsnaps his rifle and cocks it. Then he starts the engine and crunches into reverse, driving with one hand. So does Enoch. So does everyone else. One of the spotters switches on a spotlight and waves it in an arc. The elephant begins to lumber toward us. Lady Muck-on-Toast moans and tucks her head under her lord's arm. Even the Brazilians are silent and sitting down now.

"He's bluffing," says our ranger suddenly. No more than thirty seconds have passed. He lowers his rifle and stops.

I see that the elephant has indeed paused at the bank,

THE ROMANCE OF ELSEWHERE

where he is churning up dust and harrumphing like a harassed nanny. "It's O.K.," I say over my shoulder.

But the lady is not comforted. "I don't mind saying," she says, "that I blame the management for this."

We have made the road now and are driving back to camp. Behind us, the spotter mumbles something, pointing to a zebra and its foal standing in the long grass.

"I can't help thinking," Lady M-on-T continues, "that someone more competent should be put in command of people like those South Americans. Isn't it a little soon to be giving them control?"

Before leaving for America, I stop in Johannesburg. At the airport, I spot my name printed on a piece of paper and held aloft by a small African man standing in front of the Avis counter. He is Winston, my aunt's driver. My aunt is big in the Institute of Race Relations. She has told me that Winston is a Venda, with definite opinions about Mandela—that he is puffed up and unctuous, that he has opinions on everything. Certainly, he is a new sort of driver. He doesn't wear a uniform; he opens the front door of the car for me, not the back. And he radiates Old Spice.

On the way into town, I ask him about himself. He tells me that he has a wife and two children, whom he visits on the weekends. That he started out as a schoolmaster, but that now he is taking a degree in accounting, by correspondence, and working as a driver. Eventually, he says, he wants to start his own accounting firm, there is a need for black accountants, black businesses are on the rise.

So, what does he think about Mandela and the ANC? I ask.

He looks in the rearview mirror, changes lanes, turns on the air conditioning. He is sweating now, and the Old Spice has reached fever pitch. "On due consideration," he says, curling his lips around each syllable, "I'm not quite sure whether I am actually in favor."

I press him further. I tell him that I live in America and that I really want to know, I have an article to write.

"The ANC have been out of the country," he says. "Why should they come back now and tell the locals what to do?"

What, I ask, does he think they'll tell him to do?

He glances quickly at me and then back at the road. "I am still asking myself a question," he says at last. "Why, after de Klerk unbanned the ANC, did whites run out and buy guns? Will blacks be allowed to own guns now? I don't think so. And that's not fair. I hear everyone in America has got a gun."

Flying out the next day, I ask the woman sitting next to me whether she owns a gun. "We live in prisons now," she says. "Armed to the teeth. Panic buttons around our necks. Iron bars everywhere. Vicious Rottweilers. Everyone I know knows someone who's been murdered." She shakes her head. "You're much better off in America," she says.

Running the Smalls Through

BEING THE OTHER WOMAN MAY SEEM PREFERABLE TO suffering another woman, but to be woken out of a deep sleep by an enraged wife ranting in a language not one's own is to make one question the joys of illicit love at their source. This is particularly so if the culture from which the wife hails is rich in crimes of passion. And forgives them easily.

"*Ees djong man!*" the woman screamed, pointing to the man who had, somehow, slipped out of the bed we had been sharing and was standing at a safe distance in the doorway. "*Djong!*" she screamed again.

Djong? If she meant *childish*, we were certainly of a mind. But how to say this when she had the covers in her grip and was holding on to them with long, red, pointed nails?

I myself had often longed to stand just like that over a woman I had uncovered in bed with my husband. But no such opportunity had ever presented itself. Nothing, clearly, was going to spring me blameless from a marriage from which, somehow, I could imagine no other possible escape.

"I did not know," I said slowly, keeping my eyes on hers. The man in the doorway had, in fact, told me that he was divorced, and I'd had no reason to doubt him. After all, he had introduced me to his mother, taken me to lunch at his club, strolled me around the streets of his city without even a hint of concern. So that now, looking back on things, I'm not sure whether I was trying to placate a wife or an ex-wife.

"I did not know," I said again, and, for a few long seconds, she seemed to weigh the truth of this. Then, suddenly, she wheeled around and made a dash for him, and then they were both screaming down the stairs, thumping, shouting, smashing things, until, finally, a door slammed, a car started up, and there was silence.

I pulled the covers up. Despite the heat, I was shivering. How would I get out of there? Find my way to the airport? And where was I, anyway? He had brought me to the house the night before, led me through it by candlelight. See the moon on the lake? he'd said. See that hole in the wall? My brother-in-law came and shot the house.

There was no point in asking, Why the house? His whole world seemed mad to me, delightfully mad. It was the sort of madness that made sense, somehow, of my being in it at all. In its subtle shades of grey, and with him leading me up the wide curving staircase, candle held high, the house itself had seemed wild, miles from any world I would have to return to.

But now, looking around in the rude daylight, I saw walls sponge-painted in a bright mauve, cheap floral curtains, foam furniture. An old panic took hold of me, the sort of panic I have always suffered when captive in alien places. I wanted to go home.

He arrived in the doorway, heaving with sobs. "Why she do this?" he cried. "Why?"

"I want to go home, please," I said.

He came to the bed to show me ten bloody welts running down his back from shoulder to waist. "She scratch me," he wailed. "Why she do this to me?"

Until now, we had met in hotels. And even there I would often find myself wanting to go home, with him left behind, a few thousand miles behind, and me with a glass of wine and a Latin crooner on the stereo to remind myself of the romance I still had to look forward to the next time.

So why carry on? Why jeopardize a marriage, passionless and quarrelsome as it may have been, for an affair that, at best, provided only cheap hope? In fact, the question seldom occurred to me as I slipped smoothly between two, three, four versions of my life at the same time. In the version I played with him, I was a woman run through by the romantic drama of desire—the glances, the invitations, the wine. And then, once home, his sentimental protestations could sustain me even as I laughed about them with my friends. "Our love is worsted," he would say, "Our love is a violent rose."

Perhaps, after all, this first affair, and the many that followed, were nothing much more than a young and then youngish woman storing up experience against the future famine of old age—a wife, who, even if she had given up on fidelity, did not yet have the courage to give up on marriage itself.

And then, at last, I fell in love. Never mind that he had the bad teeth and bad smell of a Brit who considered bathing once a week quite sufficient to the needs of social decency, and laundering bad for his clothes. Or that he was twenty-odd years older than I, married himself, and quite accustomed, it seemed, to snatching a woman from her husband's arms to sweep her around the dance floor, leaving the husband to watch from the wings.

Once these things have begun, it is hard to know whose desire has ruled most strongly. I had seen him watching as

I danced with my husband, seen him lean forward, his lips slightly parted, slightly damp. And seeing him like that, I began to show off for him, swirling around in my four-inch Yves Saint Laurent snakeskin sandals and the sleeveless, backless dress my mother had bought me because, as she said, youth passes too quickly.

Perhaps it was she, then, who had planted in me this urgency to grab what I could while the blood still ran strong. I don't know. She herself would have been nothing but alarmed by the ever-deepening danger into which I kept putting myself. She would have cautioned me, scolded me. But, once broken, the vow of fidelity seemed to urge me on, mocking caution. I could not bear the thought of a life spent repeating itself in virtue. Everything I saw and read cried out against it, even an old woman on a beach, lamenting, "I have had two husbands and thirteen lovers, and I only regret the ones I turned down."

I can't remember now where we were that night of dancing. Austria? Switzerland? What I do remember is that we were at a conference, and that, the next day, he managed to slip into the seat next to mine on the bus before my husband could get there. And that I fell into what I can only think of now as a trance. On and on we talked, his small eyes trained on mine, and on my mouth, on my words themselves. If I said something that engaged him, he took my hand and raised it to his lips. And although I could have known how much practice had gone into all of this, still there were tears in his eyes when I said goodbye. And again when I met him a few months later at the airport.

He had come to see me on the pretext of donating sperm to a sperm bank run by one of his colleagues. Over the next few years, we met on every sort of pretext, his and mine. "Permit me to arrange it," he would say. And so I did, charmed to have the details of deception lifted so easily from my shoulders. (Some years later, sitting around a table with a group of women friends, I asked if anyone could suggest what a man could say to make himself irresistible. Everyone had something to offer, mostly predictable things—protestations of love, promises of money. And then one woman sat forward and said, "'Leave it to me.' All he needs to say is that, and I'd follow him anywhere.")

For almost two years, I permitted him to arrange my life. We would meet here or there, and, when we couldn't, we wrote letters. Oh, those years of letters! Not only his, but all of theirs. Only after my divorce did I fish them out of their hiding place—a file I'd marked "Rabelais"—and put them into a box, and the box on a shelf in my garage. And then, one day, when I went to take them out, wanting to read through all those years again, I found that the box was soaked in rat urine. So I put on a pair of rubber gloves and threw it into the garbage can.

With it went the letter that had brought things to an end. The finale itself began with his trip to Australia. Would I give him the happiness of a week in Tahiti en route? he had asked as we sipped wine, looking out over Lake Cumberland. All I had to do was to book myself onto the same flight as his; I could leave the rest to him.

But I could think of no further pretexts for leaving home, certainly not a few weeks after returning. And, anyway, I didn't want to. Dividing my life between home and lover had become a rhythm I counted on. And even though this was an affair like no other I had had—an affair that nothing, it seemed, could undo, not even when he'd come into the bathroom the night before, dangling a pair of greying Jockeys over my head as I sat in the bath, to ask if I'd run his smalls through—even so, I was not ready to go to Tahiti with him.

It was unusual for him to ask anything more than once, but this time he did. "Impossible?" he said, smiling. "Is that quite final?"

Well yes, it was. It was as final as my refusal to wash his underwear in my bathwater or anywhere else. Running the smalls through may have been what wives were expected to do, wives who were years away from being swept around a dance floor, worlds away from being asked to give a man the happiness of a week in Tahiti.

When he spoke of his wife, he did so casually, as if she were understood between us—Marjorie this, Marjorie that. Still, he asked, would I consider permitting him to set me up in a house on the English coast? Would I consider giving him that happiness?

Well no, I would not. Even in love, I was not stupid. And yet I did not think beyond the suggestion itself to the sort of man who would make it—a man who would remove a woman from her marriage only to stash her within reach of his own wife. His Marjorie. Had I given this thought, I would probably have put the matter down to the decades and cultures between us. Perhaps, after all, it was the decades and cultures that, until now, had exempted him from the natural mistrust with which I assaulted all other men in my life. Before and after him, mistrust of men could take possession of my breathing in a moment, transforming me into an inferno of suspicion and accusation. With him, however, it only crept in as I began to wonder why a pale-skinned Brit, lover of ancient places, cobbled streets, and cold, damp weather, would want to spend a week in Tahiti on his own.

I took to observing him, listening for contradictions, asking questions, trying to catch him out. But he was leagues ahead of me in this game. "Darling," he would say, "don't demean yourself in this way." "Darling," he would say, "would you be happier if I didn't go?"

And then, one evening, I noticed an airmail envelope in the inside pocket of his jacket. As soon as he was out of the room, I slipped it out—a hand-written address, a Hong Kong stamp. Quickly I pulled out the letter and opened it. And there, in bold green ink, was the word, "Darling!"

"What are you doing?" He stood in the doorway, quite still.

I hadn't heard this tone from him before. I hadn't seen his color rise in anger either. "Who is this letter from?" I said, gripping it tight.

He walked over to me and held out his hand. "This is unworthy," he said.

But my own color was rising now. "Who is it from?" I shouted, stuffing it into my pocket.

"It's from Marjorie," he said, keeping his eyes from mine.

"She's in Hong Kong? You're a liar!"

He bowed his head then. Old or *djong*, men are far more practiced in silence than women, certainly when no answer will serve.

"WHO IS SHE?"

"Don't shout, please."

But already it was as if I had only a few words left.

Already he was beginning to pull out drawers, put his clothes on the bed.

"WHO?"

"My secretary," he said, almost inaudibly.

And then something in the grey head bowed, the greying shirt, and the secretary's green ink had me rolling out the sort of noirish laugh of film that goes with lines of outrage not one's own. And even as I shouted at him, a woman longing to be restored to her own blindness, I understood how old was the farce in which I was taking part.

And when, some years later, divorced myself, I met him for lunch, thinking, "Now, surely, I shall ask myself what ever I saw in him," I was stopped at the sight of him. There he was, the grey charmer, rising to greet me with tears in his eyes. "Permit me," he said, and, "Would you give me the pleasure?" And anyone could see, even a woman heady now with the riotous, licit romp following marriage itself, that reason itself knows nothing of the heart.

Locked In

SOME YEARS AGO, I MOVED FROM SAN FRANCISCO, where I had lived for twenty years, to a small town in the wine country, an hour away. I had recently shed an unbearable marriage, sold the house I had owned with my ex-husband, and was ready for something quite new. Despite the fact that I had never lived anywhere but in the center of a city, it did not occur to me as I signed the papers on my new house that I might not be suited to life out of the swim. What I was signing on for, I decided, was Life in Middle Age: peace, privacy, and safety. At least, that's the list I presented to incredulous friends.

In fact, my quaint Victorian bungalow, surrounded by vineyards and three blocks from the center of town, has indeed become the darling of my acquaintance. They arrive from the city, ecstatic with the beauty of the journey—the hills, the vines, the cows, and the sheep. They sit on my deck under the walnut trees exclaiming on the charm of the place, how lucky I am, how clever to have moved here, etc. Swept up by their praise, I actually feel lucky, clever, confirmed in my choice. And then, when the sun begins to set, they pile into their cars and go home.

Waving one's friends back to the city, I have found, isn't all relief. Peace can be deadly, particularly when it comes in the evening, after a day in the studio. But the price of company for an evening is company for the night. Friend or lover, the guest room needs to be readied—I have always insisted on a bedroom to myself—and then, with the talk and the bustle, the next day tends to be lost for work.

Still, still there are the compensations to the country life. One doesn't need earplugs to sleep here. And the sun does shine in summer. The air is fresh. Every morning, there are birds on the lawn eating things. I have as much privacy as I want. And, until a few years after I moved in, I felt completely safe. I could walk anywhere, day and night, without city vigilance. I could leave my windows and doors open, my keys in the car. The whole arrangement seemed quaint to me. This is the way America was in the fifties, friends told me. This is how they'd grown up themselves.

And then one day, I opened the local paper and read that a rapist had attacked a woman viciously, not half a mile from my house. The woman he attacked was about my age, living alone, on this side of town. Two weeks later, two blocks away, he hit again. The town was in an uproar. Meetings were convened. Psychologists and rape counselors and locksmiths and policemen and sheriffs all had something to say. Women came forward, single women in their forties and fifties, who had this and other things in common with the victims: outdoor light bulbs unscrewed, windows broken, small items filched from their houses. The story made it into the San Francisco papers. Friends phoned in alarm and, perhaps, a little glee. Come back to the city, they said. Stay with them. And shouldn't I get a dog? A gun? Keep a lover in place?

I know that I am not a natural target, not even for panhandlers. I walk fast and determined and straight. I look fierce without even meaning to. But it is the dangers of the city that I'm used to. I know what to avoid there, and when. A serial rapist, who stalks his victims for months before hiding himself in a closet in her house, is not a danger I have ever considered before.

Now, however, I saw him in every man I passed. I came to feel watched myself. And the night took on old childish terrors. So did dark places, and odd sounds. A walnut falling onto the roof had me out of bed and all the lights on. If I came home in the dark, I didn't park in my garage. I left my outdoor lights on and checked each day that they were still screwed in. I had a fence built to close off the garden from the street, with a lock and a peephole.

Once peace was shattered, next went privacy, which was first on my list to the real estate agent who sold me the house. I realized, however, that I should know my neighbors. One set I knew already, but now I had to know them all: both sides, behind, and across the road. More than this, they had to know me. They had to have my phone number, and feel free to call if they didn't see a light on, or if they did. We met and considered banding together into a Neighborhood Watch arrangement, which would have required monthly get-togethers, like Tupperware parties, at each other's houses.

I attended meetings, swapped names and numbers with other women, women with whom I had nothing in common except fear. They phoned me with the latest information, and invited me to more meetings. I phoned the mayor and demanded to know what was being done to catch the rapist, why experts were not being called in to solve the case. There have always been rapes around here, the mayor told me. So, two more rapes, that happen to have taken place on the better side of town, are not sufficient cause for calling in experts.

When a third woman was raped and savagely beaten two blocks away, I signed up for a self-defense class. Next to me in the class sat a single woman who had had her outdoor lights tampered with, her windows broken. The policeman who came to investigate didn't report the incidents, she told me. She had bought a gun, she said. A woman on the other side told me there were rumors that the rapist was a gardener, a construction worker, even a policeman.

The rapist can be any man, said the Assault Prevention Expert, waving a can of tear gas at us. I considered the pharmacist, the mailman, the supermarket bagger, the man whose dog fouled my grass every morning. I had heard that men were afraid now to walk their dogs without their wives at their sides. I'd seen men walking down the middle of the street, staying out of shadows. I myself had walked like this. I had travelled widely on my own, all over the world, wandered the streets of Istanbul, Cairo, Rio, practicing normal caution. But never, until now, had I felt that normal caution was useless; that I could be the victim of Anyman.

"Don't be a victim," said the Expert. She handed around a Personal Security Products Catalog. She showed us the Personal Alarm, which had a ghastly shriek. Then there was a stun gun that could have a man down on the ground while you ran. But I didn't want to run. I wanted to hold the rapist down in agony until he begged for mercy. I wanted to put him into prison so that he could be raped himself.

When I got home, the house was silent and cold. I locked myself in, as I was now accustomed to do, looked into the closets, under the bed, set the alarm. Then I settled down to admire my arsenal. But, spread out on the kitchen table—fashioned in cheap black plastic, or closed into black vinyl holsters—the devices looked like dime-store junk. Also, I'd bought too many. I realized that I could only use them one at a time. And, anyway, I still didn't feel safe.

So, what would it take, I wondered, to feel safe again? If the rapist were caught, would I drive into my garage in the dark? Would I leave my front door open? Would I sit out in the sun without my Personal Alarm? In time, perhaps, I thought. In time, in fact, I did. But although I still walked straight and fierce, and could tap real fury at the thought of a stranger having the power to rob me of my peace of mind, I understood that peace and privacy could not be bought and sold. That safety was an illusion. That women were safe nowhere, and probably never had been. Not even in the fifties.

Happy Birthday to Me

WITHIN A CULTURE THAT IS REACHING BREAKING POINT in its search for a real cause for celebration, women have come up with something quite novel: themselves. *Celebrating*—twin to that other horror of modern parlance, *honoring*—attaches itself like a weed to every damp spot along the female path, birth to death. And now, several reaches beyond the halfway mark, are the fiftieth, sixtieth, seventieth birthdays.

For a whole generation of women, turning fifty is being called upon to celebrate the coming out of womanhood. Perhaps this is because for so long it signaled precisely the loss of the same. Menopause, once a tiresome, even a dreaded inevitability of middle age, has been dragged out of the closet, dusted off, tarted up, and invited to the party. Now, women, high on age, discuss their PMZ (post-menopausal zest), their newly degenerating bodies, and the men that still desire them. Goddesses are invoked. Rights are invoked. We have the right to let the inner child out, the right to cry. We are, after all, celebrating Life and the fact that we're still in it after half a century on Our Planet. Our Bodies, Our Power, the Joy of Life's Passages—for all this we feel Grateful.

Has anxiety ever run to a higher pitch in the name of celebration? Has the hysteria for public confession taken root even here, at the fiftieth birthday party? So that to utter what either goes without saying or was heretofore unutterable in the company of strangers is to be miraculously unburdened? Simply listen to the birthday speeches, the catalogues of reverses overcome—ex-husbands and other illnesses, hostile tenure committees, rebellious children. And then to the inevitable embrace of ordinary happiness that follows—the sun that shines one day at a time; the treasure of friendship, of grandchildren, of second or third husbands. Nearer, My God, to Thee, and pass the nuts, please.

Every decade brings with it its own anxiety—at twenty the madness to experience life, at thirty to establish a life, at forty to change it. But for the aging woman, beset by concerns about lasting the distance, there is now the added requirement that she looks forward rather than back, that she does so with hope, and that she does so in public.

America is not the first society to go in for mass public confessions. The Chinese were fond of them in the third century A.D., and they have popped up regularly ever since. Nor is the count-your-blessings mode of celebration new either. It is simply that when one of life's true milestones is colonized by any group and turned into a mass coming-out, then the milestone itself is trivialized in the process. And privacy, already radically undermined in our culture, shrinks further toward the horizon.

Perhaps my antipathy toward such trumped-up celebration stems, in part, from the fact that I grew up in the buck-up, grin-and-bear-it, pull-up-your-socks culture of a once-British colony. Both at school and at home, the mawkish and the sentimental would bring on gales of derision. Let anyone be foolish enough to lapse into self-pity and she would be pounced on with caricature and exaggerated sympathy. Even at home, where my mother, an actress, threw herself regularly into tragic poses, we simply rolled our eyes, or just ignored her completely. If it didn't bring her out of it—if her fits and sulks kept the whole family on edge—at least we had the satisfaction of letting her know that we were not taken in.

Not even she, however, would have dreamed of dramatizing anything as normal as menopause. In a house composed largely of women, the only nod made in the direction of female biology was an incinerator my father had installed in the servants' yard to dispose of the plethora of soiled sanitary towels. For the rest—cramps, quick tempers, tears— these were to be ignored, or, if not ignored, considered in the same category as bad weather. To hold a ceremony celebrating a girl's first menstrual period would have been as unthinkable as sacrificing a virgin to the moon.

By the same token, menopause was considered a family inconvenience—windows to be opened, fans fetched, and so forth. The decades came and went. Sometimes, when one turned into the next, there would be a particularly large party, usually for my father. Because my mother was a few years older than he, she kept her decades to herself until, when she turned eighty, she had no choice: we threw the party for her. Forty or fifty members of our large family came, as well as a number of friends going back to my mother's youth and even to her childhood.

Perhaps, if extended families were still intact, the milestone birthdays themselves would be back where they once belonged—within the family and close acquaintance. There the journey makes sense, with the past and the future all around us in the persons of those who went before, those who accompanied us, and those who will follow. Now, however, it is often friends who take the place of family, who flatten out the whole idea of generation, who conspire, somehow, to banish all thought of the certainty of death. Friends give us the parties, or they enjoin us to give them for ourselves. Fifty, sixty, seventy and loving life to bits.

Some years ago, at my first experience of such a party, I had no idea at all that there was a birthday involved, certainly not a fiftieth birthday. I was a new acquaintance of the hostess, who was herself new in town. And I would never have imagined that this woman—sophisticated, successful, intelligent—would have agreed to such an event. But there she was in the corner of her living room, opening gift after gift, blushing like a bride-to-be. She slipped the cards into the boxes and then handed them to the friend sitting at her feet.

Men looked in, putting on a show of interest. But men have been turning the decades in triumph for centuries. For them, women jump out of cakes, wives grow fearful. Here, on the other hand, was a woman of substance, giggling about a gift plonked into her lap by the giver, the friend at her feet, who was around fifty herself. There was whispered debate as to whether the gift should be opened at all in public. Yes. No. Yes.

Sexy underwear, I thought, oh dear God. All around the room hung photographs of the hostess as a young woman, a very beautiful young woman. Clearly, although it is an important creed of the new cult of celebration to find the fifty-year-old even more beautiful than, say, the twenty-year-old—evidence of life lived, the spirit settled, etc.—the message wasn't quite selling.

Off came the bow, then the wrapping. The company fell silent as she lifted the gift out of the box. It was a book after all, only a book. But then she clutched it to her bosom. She laughed, embarrassed at last. So did the friend at her feet and a few women around them. Even the men looked interested now. And then the hostess turned the book around to face the audience. It was *Listening to Prozac*.

✱

SOON AFTER I turned fifty, a routine mammogram showed evidence of breast cancer. Sitting on the examining table, waiting for my initial examination by the surgeon, I was startled when a woman walked into the room. She was not the surgeon, not even a nurse. She was about my age, bleached and teased and sprayed, and smiling with frightening determination. "Hi!" she said. "Mind if I sit down?"

I did mind. It was all I could do to keep from losing control myself, and I didn't want a stranger there to see me if I did.

She handed me a flier. "Hi!" she said again, unsure, perhaps, as to whether I spoke English.

I nodded, taking the flier.

"Well," the woman said, "isn't it a lovely day?"

At this point, her false cheer began to do its work. A lovely day for cancer, I thought, cheering up a bit. Had a friend been with me, we might even have managed a laugh.

"Well," the woman said again, "I've come to tell you that you are not alone. Did you realize how many support groups we have out there?" She gestured out into the world, still smiling intrepidly.

I stared at her. I was as alone in my life as I had ever been. My father had just died, my mother had sunk into senile dementia, my lover had decamped, and the college at which I taught would not allow me the six weeks I needed for radiation. I was reliant completely on my daughter and my two closest friends. And even so, it was as if a glass wall separated me from everyone, everyone in the world who did not have cancer. Still, joining a group, any group, especially one composed of strangers who had nothing more in common than breast cancer, was inconceivable to me.

I am no good at Group, any group, even one promising hope. Nor can I stand a parade, militant causes, causes of any stripe. Pink brooches, yellow bangles, armbands, T-shirts—any badge of right-mindedness sends me right back to the cultural shudder with which I grew up.

I handed back the flier with thanks.

As it happened, I had turned fifty with great relief. A bad marriage was behind me, my daughter was finally out of her teens and becoming bearable, I had a man who made me laugh, my books were being published, I was free to run my own life.

And then, soon behind, came the shock. Until that point, I had often pondered the torque between the allure and the terror of death. Having grown up in the wake of the Holocaust, in a family that felt itself saved from it by a mere trick of history, I had stood on the edge of that mysterious, horrifying terrain, staring in, wondering how and whether I would have survived myself.

And now here, at last, was the knock at the door: statistics, percentages, informed guesses, groups of fellow sufferers. Quite soon, I came to understand that any allure death might have held for me until now was a sentimental indulgence. I didn't want to die. After surgery and radiation, when I was given my life back, I was filled with uncomplicated relief.

But I conducted no celebrations; I am far too superstitious for that. What I longed for as much as I had ever longed for anything was the peace of a simple life. I kept returning to an image of two rooms overlooking the sea. All the excesses of life—things, people—would be jettisoned. I would savor my time as I had squandered it before. I would consider the present as once I had considered the future.

What I failed to consider in this fantasy was myself—that, mutatis mutandis, the person I was at fifty was the same as the one who had gone before. And that the life of peace I had imagined I wanted would quite possibly have felt like death itself. Perhaps it was simply that I did not have the strength of character for such denial, that the wisdom of peace and simplicity was not my portion. Whatever the case, I feel sure that I would soon have begun acquiring back the things and the circle of acquaintance that I had jettisoned, filling my rooms and my life with them again, even as I continued to long for peace and simplicity.

✳

AND STILL I am disinclined to celebrate what I do not consider to be an achievement. Which is not to say that I am not glad to have been spared. I am, I am. One needs only to visit an old cemetery to see the tombstones of women who died in childbirth before reaching the age of twenty-five to understand that fifty is a lucky thing to be. And even if twenty-five itself is not what it once was—how many parents have their twenty-five-year-olds back in the house with a college degree and no job?—nor, indeed, is fifty.

A fifty-year-old woman is no longer an old woman, even in our youth-mad culture. There is still life in her. Certainly there is spending power.

And so, if she can handle the jump in her health insurance premiums, join the AARP with insouciance, shed her girlish little voice, and resist the pull of merchandisers of every stripe, including those of the medical profession, to move her backward in time and dignity—if she can sidestep the determination of her fellow celebratees to make a virtue of an inevitability, and can emerge into middle age with the wisdom and dignity that should go with the territory—if she can do all this, then, indeed, this aging woman might have something to celebrate.

Ignorance Chic

THERE IS IGNORANCE AND THERE IS IGNORANCE CHIC.
I practice both. Half my life I have pretended to know who
and what people are talking about (ignorance). And the
other half I have pretended not to (chic). Some years ago,
sitting in the office of an editor in chief, both halves came
into eclipse.

In burst an assistant, almost without knocking.
Someone whose name sounded like "Karioka" was put out
and demanding a first-class ticket to Saint Petersburg. "We
don't give first-class tickets," said the editor in chief, put
out herself. But the assistant, clearly battered by Karioka at
the other end, stood her ground. The intimation was that
Karioka wouldn't go at all if not first class and what then?

The editor in chief sighed, slammed a pen down,
raised her eyebrows at me. Can you believe this? the look

said. I shook my head. Really I couldn't. Except that I was wondering how Karioka was doing it. I, too, have had fits on occasion, but never in the direction of first-class tickets. Two other editors came in. I listened with interest to the talk of upgrade certificates, calling in markers with the airlines. The editor in chief might be put out, but she didn't want to lose Karioka for this mission, whatever it was. Out went the assistant, slightly cheered. And then the editor in chief exploded. "Prima donnas!" she boomed. "Can you believe it?"

Again I said no, I couldn't. Nor could the other editors. None of us could believe it. "Who's Karioka?" I asked.

Shrieks, cackles. So delighted were they that no one bothered to answer my question. I didn't mind. I'd made a hit, more of a hit than Karioka, whoever she was. And I'd cheered them all up.

I also seemed to have raised my own worth. And had done so in the best possible way—unintentionally (the highest form of ignorance chic). Just as natural style in dress wins out every time over received style, so really not knowing has the edge over pretending not to know.

Even standard ignorance chic, however, is a fine conversational weapon in the face of the snob and the sycophant. Or on behalf of the intimidated. The English have been practicing it for eons. Diana who? The Rolling what?

In my case, the practice on all fronts is helped by what passes for an English accent and a manner and style that fall into place accordingly. And also by a natural insouciance for celebrities, for popular culture, and for received cultural shibboleths. I turn my head, I turn the page, I turn the dial.

Take NPR, for instance, and its "knowledgeable sources." I grew up with radio; this is not radio. The announcers sound like Montessori teachers, and the program sponsors like God handing down the Ten Commandments to Charlton Heston. In the company of NPR worshippers, there is sport to be had in mentioning that one does not listen to it, that perhaps commercial talk radio is more entertaining (with a cup of instant coffee and a cigarette, perhaps?). Or that one skips past the Op-Ed page in the paper. That the word itself—*Op-Ed*—is irritating. As are the sort of people given to dropping it into a conversation as if they were citing Herodotus.

To my surprise, owning up to these aversions at the right moment is tantamount to ignorance chic. (Terry who? On fresh what?) People tend to assume one might be given to higher forms of opinion-gathering. *The Wall Street Journal*? (Full of surprises.) *The Nation*? (Quality opinions.) *The TLS*? (See "Op-Ed.") *National Enquirer*? (Tee-hee chic.)

As to basic ignorance, there are some subjects that are as boring to know about as not to know about—driverless cars, social media, green drinks, #anything, pregnant celebrities. And there are others which—unless one is in that small, self-selected group that has turned ignorance on its head—are downright lowbrow. Confusing George Eliot with George Sand is decidedly not chic. Nor—unless one can do it well—Monet with Manet. Ditto Cornell with Oscar Wilde.

No. Ignorance chic is best employed as a natural antidote to cultural fundamentalism and the hegemony of the media. It is the ultimate put-down—the blank stare, the apologetic shrug, the stifled yawn. It is the mispronunciation. It is getting the name just wrong. And it's nothing new. Remember Hermione Gingold asking Dick Cavett, "Zsa Zsa who?" Go out and do likewise.

Letter from Texas

SO IT WAS BACK TO DIPS AND CHIPS ON A SATURDAY night, and Marvin Gaye with the carpet rolled up. Not to mention dial telephones, metal desks, electric bells, adds and drops, "lay" for "lie," falafel for lunch, poster shops, incense vendors, more electric bells, teaching the unteachable, grading the ungradable—the whole baggage, in short, of my new and temporary patron, the Academy.

Had marriage been that bad? Remind me, please.

At least then I'd only had to walk downstairs to go to work. And, when I did venture out, it wasn't by way of a thruway called "MoPac." One try at MoPac and I settled for the long route to the university past E-Z Pawn and Goodwill. MoPac needed attitude, Texas style—men who were men sealed into cars with darkened windows; women in pickups, cinched and crimped and sprayed. Try to get on and they'd speed up. Stick to the speed limit and they'd nose right up from behind and then blast you with the horn. Turn on the radio and you'd hear Willie Nelson singing, "Don't Mess with Texas." The other thruway, IH-35, was worse. Those were Minnesotans on their way to Mexico. And this place was lost in the crease of the Rand McNally map.

I'd always thought Australia would be like this—full of sky, and, on the ground, flat, square, boxy houses on flat, square plots. Here and there a vast, open tract sprouting scrub and a shack of corrugated iron. People dressed like extras, in those hats and boots. Plagues of insects. "Townhome complexes" with names like "Versailles" and "Saint-Tropez" nestled among malls and strung together by a series of MoPacs. Up in the hills, suburban houses closer to the sky. And, under God, the abiding motif of sport and beer.

"Ma'am, I just want you to know I'm shootin' for an A," said a C student suffering from television ear. ("Son, I'm leaving." "But, Dad, think of Mom. Think of what this will do to her." "I am thinking of your mother, son. Trust me. One day you will be old enough to understand.") He was taking my "Creative Writing: Fiction" class "to better sharpen his verbal skills." The fact was, said he, he was headed for law school. He needed the hours and he needed the grades.

I wondered what my life would have been like if I'd gone to law school. Down the corridor I noticed Famous Indian Writer rounding the bend, with a woman student in pursuit. Recently, he'd made it big with a television series in India based on some of his novels.

"BUT DIDN'T THE INDIANS EVER RISE UP AND REVOLT LIKE THE BLACKS DID HERE?" the student shouted at him.

Famous Indian Writer was very old and quite deaf. He waved a hand gamely in the air and shuffled into his office. I wandered down to say hello. He, too, was there as a visiting writer. He welcomed me in, although he was still not quite sure who I was. His office was always filled with women in saris talking all at once. This one was a daughter, that one was someone else. They all lived in a furnished apartment near the university. His life seemed like a festival, untouched by Texas. MoPac didn't come into it. And he was quite amused at the very idea of teaching.

"WHAT ARE YOU DOING ABOUT GRADING?" I shouted.

"I'm teaching them my own books," he shouted back. "Either they ask me questions or they don't."

I made my way back home in the spirit of an outcast. It was ninety-five degrees. My car had no air conditioning, and my townhome was infested with crickets. So was the one across the pool. My friend the handyman had told me that the redhead who lived there was a medical student and had two diaphragms under her bed, one on each side, both of which he'd sprayed for crickets.

Gazing across the pool, with its dozens of crickets skittering on the surface, I wondered how things would have been if I were a doctor. The redhead was home a lot, and men came and went there all the time. One wore an army uniform and carried a ghetto blaster. Another wore Bermuda shorts and a baseball cap turned around backward. The redhead herself drove a white Corvette, and, judging by the fights I'd overheard, also suffered from television ear. None of which, of course, militated against her being a medical student, but someone told me that there wasn't a medical school anywhere near there.

The handyman had said she drank a lot of beer, and that she'd sidled up to him and made pointed suggestions. But he'd had a heart attack, and the manager of the townhome complex, who'd survived being shot through the head by her ex-husband, was driving him round the bend. She kept falling onto her knees and praising the Lord, trying to win him over to her church. The handyman, however, came from Boston, not Texas. He was a Roman Catholic. And who should know more about God than he did?

Yom Kippur was coming up. For the first time in years, I felt homesick for Jews. I decided to phone the Hillel Society to find out about services for the unaffiliated.

"You need an ah-dee," the girl said.

"What kind?" I had nothing that certified me as a Jew. But anything seemed possible down there. A cricket landed on the phone book and waved its feelers at me.

"Student ah-dee," she said, "Or else there's a donation."

"I'm faculty," I replied. It didn't sound bad, after all. "Will that do?"

"Fine," she said, "no donation."

"What time's the Kol Nidrei service?" I asked.

"The whaaat?"

"Kol Nidrei!" In my twenty years in America, I'd never had so much trouble making myself understood.

"Kooltree?"

"KOL NIDREI," I barked. "K-O-L N-I-D-R-E-I."

"'Scuse me, ma'am," she said, "I'm not Jewish, I just answer the phone."

The cricket took off and landed on the sugar bowl. I reached down slowly for my shoe. The handyman had said he'd put some screening over the air conditioning vents to stop the crickets getting in, but he hadn't been there on Friday, and I glanced across the pool, wondering about his heart. And whether my absence at the department picnic would be noticed on Saturday. I thought of middle-aged men with tenure heaping potato salad onto paper plates, and of Oscar Wilde heaping scorn on the head of his tutor. I reminded myself to quote Wilde to my class on Tuesday. I had written the words down and stuck them with Post-it tape to the walls of the townhome:

"Nothing that is worth knowing can be taught."

Doing No Harm

Some Thoughts on Reading and
Writing in the Age of Umbrage

DURING THE DARKEST DAYS OF APARTHEID, I WAS invited onto a morning television talk show in the San Francisco Bay Area, to appear there with a black South African writer. His memoir had recently been brought into the light by Oprah Winfrey, and he was now on the circuit with the mass-market paperback. It seemed obvious to me as to why they wanted me on the show: I was white; I'd grown up under apartheid, and I was to be held to account for its injustices and sufferings.

"I can't do it," I said to my editor.

"But you *must*," she said. "It's wonderful exposure. And it's been far too long since your last book."

My last book, published three years before, had been an autobiographical novel about a Jewish girl growing up in a rather eccentric theatrical family in South Africa in the fifties and sixties. The book had garnered respectable reviews and caused outrage in South Africa, where the government considered a few semi-sexual scenes between white and black dangerously provocative. So they'd canceled my appearances at local universities, and on radio and television.

To be put on display again, now that all that was behind me—to be paraded out this time as the child of privilege, having to face off against a victim of such privilege—well, no, I wouldn't do it.

"Do you know," said the editor, "how many millions watch this show?"

Thousands or millions, it would only make the thing worse. "Can't they find someone else?" I said.

She sighed. "We'd like you to do this," she said impatiently, "and we'll be disappointed if you don't. But, if you're adamant, of course there's nothing we can do."

✳

AT 6 A.M., I arrived at the television station and was ushered quickly into the green room. The other writer was there already, staring at a television monitor on which a geron-tologist was chatting amiably about geriatric incontinence. In a ribbon along the bottom of the screen ran, A WORLD OF DIFFERENCE: BLACK HISTORY MONTH, and then, NEXT: A JEWISH WOMAN DESCRIBES HER EXPERIENCE GROWING UP UNDER APARTHEID IN SOUTH AFRICA.

Jewish woman? I leaned forward to look more closely. But the gerontologist was winding up now, shaking hands, leaving the screen. And a young man had arrived to shep-herd us both from the green room and out into the blinding light of the stage.

There I sat, hardly breathing, as the microphone was clipped on, tested, reclipped. For over a week, my friends had been rehearsing me: If they ask you this, say that. If they accuse you of that, just say this. I'd written it all down, read it in the bath every night, and then again before going to bed. But, somehow, neither the questions nor the answers would stick. The minute I read them, I forgot them.

As it happens, I am at my most useless when rehearsed. Had I gone in without trying so hard to be prepared—straining for phrases, ideas, arguments that were not my own—I might have saved myself at least this terror. But, in the event, I sat as if carved in rock, my back straight, and a look of gravity on my already-grave face.

The interviewer gave a practiced smile. She held up first the other writer's book, and then my own. "Ongoing racial injustices faced by those who grew up in South Africa," she was saying. "Devastating poverty, horrors of growing up under apartheid rule—these made for difficult, if not impossible childhoods as our next guests know first-hand. They both survived growing up in this country—she, a white Jewish female, and he a black male."

Survived? I tried to take the words in, but they only seemed to hum around my head like flies. And the stage was a furnace. This must be what a stroke is like, I thought, looking around for someone, some sort of audience to give me my bearings. From the stage, however, it was impossible to work out just who the real audience was—the live audience out there, somewhere in the dark? the interviewer? the enormous eye of the camera turning this way and that like a Cyclops?

And then, suddenly, I remembered. One of my friends, a woman entirely comfortable on television shows, had already given me the answer. The camera is the real audience, she'd said, but you must *never* look at it, never. You look only at the interviewer, as if you don't even see a camera.

The trouble with this was that the interviewer was ever more painful to look at. She was a hopeless actress—opening her eyes too wide, scrinching and scrunching her face into an exaggerated look of sorrow as the other writer talked.

"We slept on pieces of cardboard under the kitchen table," he was saying. "Sirens blaring, dogs barking . . . We had to scavenge for half-eaten sandwiches—"

He wasn't much good at this himself, delivering the lines too quickly, and in a high-pitched, self-righteous singsong.

The interviewer sighed. She shook her head.

"The only solace we children had," he went on, "was that each night my mother would gather us around the fire and tell some beautiful stories."

"And we," the interviewer broke in, "go home and watch television." She held his book sadly up to the camera.

I'd seen this sort of show before, usually while flipping through channels in hotel rooms. Regardless of the offenses being aired, there was something in the parading of suffering as entertainment—the bid for sympathy, the performance of the sympathy itself—shallow, sentimental, short-lived—something in all this that left the heart defiant.

Considering this now, as they talked, I was thinking that the paradox applied in just the same way to self-pity or self-righteousness on the page. And, for a moment, I almost managed to forget what I was there for myself.

"Lynn?"

I looked up.

"You were growing up in South Africa at the same time," said the interviewer, the smile back in place.

Here we go, I thought.

"Yes," I said, trying not to look at the camera. But there, on a small monitor attached to it, was my face staring back at me—sober, somber, worthy of Mount Rushmore—and LYNN FREED, RAISED IN SOUTH AFRICA running beneath it.

She sat forward. "But certainly, it couldn't have been as horrible?"

"No, of course not," I said. "It couldn't have been more different. I grew up in a large house, with loving parents, servants, a measure of ease and freedom—"

"But you also experienced some *difficulties*?" she cut in quickly.

"Difficulties?" I said.

"Because you are *Jewish*?"

I frowned at her. Never mind that I couldn't conjure up any of the answers I'd tried to memorize; this was entirely the wrong question.

"No," I said. "Whatever difficulties I experienced were trivial in comparison with his." And then, because this didn't seem to satisfy her, I added, "Probably much the same as those of any Jewish child growing up in an Anglo-Saxon society."

She blinked. She reached for my book and held it up. LYNN FREED, RAISED IN SOUTH AFRICA ran again along the bottom of the screen. But her smile seemed to have frozen in place and she with it. I saw that she was wearing an earphone, and that beads of sweat were beginning to stand out on her forehead.

I glanced at the other writer. He, too, was sweating under the heat of the lights. So was I.

"Okay!" said the interviewer suddenly. "Back in a moment!"

With that, the lights went up in the auditorium and, yes, there was the real audience out there. They were raked almost to the ceiling—a sea of women chatting, shuffling, gazing down at the stage.

"*Lynn!*" A large blond woman with a clipboard had rushed at me out of nowhere, hair and eyes wild.

I looked up at her.

"This was not *at all* what we *expected* you to say!" she hissed, panting.

"What?"

"I'm the *producer!*" she said.

The producer? For the moment, I couldn't think what a producer was, or why this should matter to me. But, whatever she was, I felt as if I were failing my orals. Or had been stopped for speeding on the highway.

"What *did* you expect me to say?" I whispered urgently.

"We want you to talk about being *discriminated* against, as a *Jewish* girl!" she said furiously, very flushed in the face.

"But that was not at *all* the case!" I was reddening in anger now myself. "It was *my* sort of parents who employed *his* sort of parents, for God's sake! It's all in the book."

"Agh!" she said, consulting the clipboard. "*We don't have time to read the books!*"

✱

RECENTLY, IN A creative writing course I was teaching, I found myself facing a standoff between two of the students. One was a rather beefy athlete and the other, whom I'll call Alice, a woman who had once been a man. The contention was over a story the athlete had written, in which men have been magically turned into women, dogs stand up on their hind legs and talk, and so forth. At a certain point in this story, one of the newly minted women looks down disconsolately to where once had been the pride of his (or her) manhood and feels disempowered, "empty," airy.

The class, most of whose members were devotees of fantasy fiction, was quite taken with it all. But then up spoke Alice. She was offended, she said, *very* offended.

What's more, she had compiled a list of the offenses, which she then proceeded to work through, taking over the class.

Over the years, I have had to defuse any number of such standoffs in the face of offended sensibilities, although never until now on the score of sex. Usually I would do this by fiat: No grandstanding! The story will be discussed on its own merits, and the author not held to account for writing about racists, idiots, perverts, and so on.

All this the students knew. They knew, too, how I felt about the stranglehold of political correctness in a creative writing class, or in any class, for that matter—that it had no place there, trigger warnings and safe spaces notwithstanding. They would have heard me quote E. L. Doctorow, who said, "I believe nothing of any beauty or truth comes of a piece of writing without the author's thinking he has sinned against something—propriety, custom, faith, privacy, tradition, political orthodoxy, historical fact, or indeed, all the prevailing community standards together."

In this case, however, Alice clearly considered the sin to lie so far out of bounds, and herself so qualified to address it from both sides of the issue, that she felt entitled to teach us all a lesson in right thinking. Indeed, as she worked through the points on her list—empowerment, disempowerment, victimization, and so forth—the class fell into a sort of guilty silence, casting down their eyes or glancing, occasionally, over at me. The athlete, in the meanwhile, bleated weakly, here and there, that he hadn't meant to offend anyone; it was just an idea he'd had, a sort of joke—

Some years ago, the New York State Regents English Exams were discovered to contain excerpts from the works of well-known writers, almost all of which had been sanitized wholesale, and without permission. This had been done, explained a commissioner, to comply with "sensitivity guidelines," and in order that no student be "uncomfortable in a testing situation." To these ends, the word *hell* had been changed to *heck*, *skinny* to *thin*, *fat* to *heavy*; whole sections of a Chekhov story had been removed; Isaac Bashevis Singer cleansed of all references to Jews and Gentiles, and so on.

Is it any wonder then that, in such a world, my student, working down her list of offenses, should have felt so entitled to her discomfort? Or the writer himself so obliged to apologize?

"Okay," I said, breaking into the litany, "that's quite enough."

They looked up, startled. Generally, I would let them have their say before taking over.

"I am a Jew," I said. "And if I chose to be offended by every writer who describes Jews unflatteringly, I'd have to avoid Chaucer, Shakespeare, Dickens, Trollope, Pound, T. S. Eliot, Dostoevsky, and any number of others, not to mention Isaac Bashevis Singer and Philip Roth."

Silence, dead silence. What shocked them, I knew, was not Chaucer, Shakespeare, etc., but the word *Jew*, unsoftened by an *ish*. To be Jewish in this new world of ours is one thing, but to be a *Jew*—well, no, that was far too close to the ghetto.

"So now," I said, "we'll simply discuss this story."

Almost immediately, things loosened up. Someone pointed out that it's all very well to switch genders—I had failed completely in getting them to use the words *sex* and *gender* correctly—but the dogs in the athlete's story all seemed to talk like teenage boys. The discussion lightened into laughter. In fact, for the rest of our weeks together, a sort of lightness took hold of the whole class, Alice included. She laughed along, seeming to forget entirely the heavy role in which she'd cast herself. And, in so doing, she became rather beloved of the others.

They were young, most in their early twenties, and few, if any, I thought, would become writers. The issue of corruption—the corruption of the imagination by the constraints of right-mindedness—posed little danger to literature from them. And, anyway, their imaginations, their thinking, their use of the language itself, was already well on the way to corruption. They were students at an English-speaking university, in a country of English-speaking universities, where talks such as the following were commonly on offer in the humanities:

"Women's Self-Perpetuated Oppression: Complicity and Moral Responsibility in Collective Action Problems."

"The 'Illegal Alien': Intersectionality, Biopolitical Racism, and the Construction of Immigrant Subjectivity."

"Quasi-Metaphoricity and the Turning Force of Alterity."

Comedy Central? *Saturday Night Live*? Not at all. These conglomerations are what passes for the language of scholarship. And, as it turned out, the students themselves seemed quite well versed in it. Perhaps they took its meaning on faith, not expecting to be able to understand it in any standard way. What they also understood quite well, I found, was the value of oppression in their cultural universe. And so the subjects of their stories were often victims—of bullying, of incest, of poverty, racism, unfairness of every sort. It was difficult to convince them that life is unfair, and that the *intention* of the writer, moral or otherwise, is irrelevant to the success of the story. That the real currency of value, the moral currency of literature, if you will, lies in the just use of the words themselves in the quest for truth.

I was not, of course, making a plea for the sort of language to be found in the self-conscious, carefully crafted prose that can seem to pass for high literary achievement. Seldom, when reading such prose, do I find myself able to forget the writer. In fact, I suspect, one is not meant to be able to forget him or her. There she is behind every clever phrase or metafictional trick—there he is delivering careful photographic descriptions of an attic, a train circa 1939, an American suburban street. Look at me! the writing shouts. See how observant I am? How significant? How clever?

And then I think yet again of Thomas Mann saying, "There are many forms of stupidity, and cleverness is the worst."

And so I try to find stories that seem to leap into existence off the half shell—stories in which the writer seems so inextricably woven into the fabric of the fiction that one can forget, as Somerset Maugham puts it, that it is a story one is reading and not a life one is living. I try to find stories that neither sanctify victimhood nor labor to serve received standards of rectitude.

So I might suggest Marguerite Duras—in particular, the way she explores the story of her first love affair as a very young, very poor white girl in French Indochina with a much older, very rich Chinese man. In many books, over her entire writing life, Duras wrote versions of this story, most recently in *The North China Lover*, published in 1992 when she was seventy-eight:

*He's Chinese. A tall Chinese. He has the white skin of the North
Chinese. He is very elegant. He has on the raw silk suit and
mahogany-coloured English shoes young Saigon bankers wear.*

In *The Lover*, her forty-eighth book, published to great
acclaim when she was seventy, she describes him thus:

> *He smells pleasantly of English cigarettes, expen-
> sive perfume, honey, his skin has taken on the scent
> of silk, the fruity smell of silk tussore, the smell of
> gold, he's desirable. I tell him of this desire.*

But, thirty years before that, when she was thirty-
six, Duras wrote a far-less-flattering portrait of him in
The Sea Wall:

> *His face was certainly not handsome, nor was his fig-
> ure. His shoulders were narrow, his arms were short . . .
> When he stood up, his ugliness became apparent.*

And, in one of her notebooks, begun when she was
almost thirty, she went even further:

> [He] *was perfectly laughable . . . He looked ridiculous because
> he was so short and thin and had droopy shoulders . . . Not*

once did I agree to walk a hundred yards with him in a street.
If a person's capacity for shame could be exhausted, I would
have exhausted mine with [him] . . . The mouth, the saliva,
the tongue of that contemptible creature had touched my lips.

DOES IT MATTER, I ask, which depiction is most just to
the original experience? Does the original experience—*if,*
indeed, the notebooks are faithful to that experience—
matter at all? Of course it does not, I say. What matters
here—what matters in all writing, in any genre—is not the
life of the writer that may or may not lie behind the work at
hand, but the life *in* that work, with all its inbuilt contradictions, its "significant irrelevancies," as Henry Green put it.
And for this there is no formula.

In all these books, Duras herself seems to be on a voyage
of discovery, moving around and through the central experience of her life, realizing it in fiction most magnificently in
The Lover—wild, furious, oblique, contradictory, true.

"The writer . . ." wrote Flannery O'Connor, "sees his
obligation as being to the truth of what can happen in life,
and not to the reader—not to the reader's taste, not to the
reader's happiness, not even to the reader's morals."

I read this to the students.

But never mind O'Connor; at least one of them is
bound to be offended by Duras. In a culture of grievance,

they have found, the victim walks at the front of the parade. And so offense will be taken on behalf of the lover, whether flatteringly or unflatteringly described. Is Duras entitled to his character? they want to know. After all, he is Chinese and the girl is white. And what about the family of impoverished white colonials, clinging ruthlessly to their last shreds of status among the natives? Racism there, too? And the domestic abuse? The mother virtually prostituting her own child? The avaricious, opium-addicted, violent brother who beats the girl up? Even the girl herself, both victim and perpetrator? Shouldn't she be judged complicit? Or is she simply the sad prey of an evil system run by evil, evil human beings?

Looked at through the prism of offense, literature is rich in subjects for discussion. It is the rare writer who hasn't found himself, at some point in his career, drawn into discussing his work in terms of its social or political significance. Making a feint toward truth-on-the-page reflecting truth-in-life can seem deliberately to be veering things off the path of righteousness. Anyway, for those with a firm toehold on the moral high ground, the complexities and contradictions inherent in the truth are not particularly interesting.

"[Political correctness]," said Doris Lessing, "is a continuation of Communist party doctrine. It's the same attitude—the need to control literature by an ideology. But the interesting thing is the people who are politically correct don't seem to recognize this . . . They haven't, as far as I can make out, taken the trouble to find out what terrible results it's had in the past, like destroying literature all over the Communist world."

Destruction apart, writing "correctly"—which is to say, endeavoring to eliminate all cause for offense—is by far the most difficult sort of writing to undertake. It is to run the story, or the essay, or the memoir—or whatever one is attempting—through an ever more crowded minefield, a crooked path at best. And this metaphor does not take into account the skill it takes to negotiate a real minefield. What it takes to write the sort of bland, flat, predictable, charmless prose that tells the reader only what she approves of already is a deadening of the mind and heart, a stilling of the desire for truth, without which desire nothing good can ever be written.

*

ONCE, IN THE mid-eighties, riding on a bus down Fifth Avenue with my editor, I was telling her about a book I had found recently in a bookstore in South Africa. It was entitled *An Easy Zulu Vocabulary and Phrase Book*, and subtitled,

Simple Sentences for Use in the Home and Garden and on Other Everyday Occasions. The book had been published in 1938 by a respectable publisher of textbooks in South Africa and was now in its fourth edition, umpteenth printing.

"The primary object of this little work," said the preface, "is to help newcomers in their common contacts with Zulus." To this end, the phrases provided were mostly in the imperative: *Come here, Answer when I call you, Wipe the table, Do not smear your clothes with blood,* etc.

The editor was predictably outraged. "You *must* write this up!" she said.

And, as soon as I returned to California, I sat down to do so. Day after day I struggled. After a while, just *thinking* about how to find my way into a subject with what I knew to be the appropriate tone of outrage seemed to guarantee that nothing would take life. Still, I persevered, draft after draft of predictable, lifeless, self-righteous nonsense.

And then, one day, just as I was about to give up, I landed on an opening sentence. "White South Africans," I wrote, "are convinced that having servants is no easy matter." Away went all thoughts of pleasing the editor—and, behind her, the whole, vast outrageable audience whom I had hoped to serve.

From then on, I wrote quickly, one ironic leap to the next, as if in the interests of explaining that world to this.

Taking this tone, coming at the thing from behind, allowed the book, those commands, and that whole complicated world to speak for themselves. It also, and not incidentally, allowed the reader to laugh.

The piece built up to a finale in a picnic vignette from a section in the book entitled "Motoring."

We will stop here.
We will have some lunch.
Make a fire.
Put the kettle on.
Spread the rug in the shade.
Get out the lunch basket.
See how deep the river is.

"Useful Zulu Phrases" was my first publication in *Harper's Magazine*.

✱

SOME YEARS AGO, a poet I knew told the story of a class she was teaching in Southern California. In this class was an old woman who had survived Auschwitz. She was writing about it, but her poems were a failure. They were simply litanies of horror, suffering, misery, all in the abstract, all sounding as if they had been told many times before. In one poem, the survivor wrote of children being led to their deaths. And, indeed, the members of the class responded with phrases of horror and outrage. But nothing in the poem seemed more real than the idea itself—no images, no phrases, nothing that made the blood run cold.

"Tell me," said the teacher, "what you saw when those children were being led past you. Tell me what you heard."

The survivor shook her head. "We couldn't see because there was a wall," she said. "And we couldn't hear because of the geese."

"Geese?" said the teacher.

"Oh yes," said the survivor. "The Germans kept a flock of geese. They beat them so that they would honk, and we couldn't hear the children crying as they led them to the gas chamber."

So, there was the poem. And the class was, at last, in tears.

When Enough Is Enough

Age and the Creative Impulse

SOME YEARS AGO, A GOOD FRIEND WAS ASKED BY THE *Paris Review* to conduct one of their long interviews with a much older, much venerated writer. She's done her best work, said the *Review* editor, so it's time to interview her.

I was not yet old myself when I heard this story, but it stayed with me, a sort of memento mori with its sweeping surety, the surety of a dairy farmer surveying his cows with dog food in mind. Would such an editor, I wondered, have fingered Yeats during what might have been considered a career lull? Before, say, he came to his wonderful poems of old age?

Recently, I read a very good novel by a prolific British novelist of whom I'd never heard. It was the writer's twelfth novel, published when she was seventy-eight. I loved it, and went on to read its companion novel, also good, published three years later. So then I went in search of her earlier novels, reading through three of them before I gave up. Certainly, they were accomplished, elegant, cleverly wrought. But they lacked what her last two novels had so brilliantly achieved: the feeling, as Somerset Maugham put it, that it was not a story one was reading, but a life one was living.

Molly Keane, the late Irish writer, is such another. She wrote eleven novels and a few plays under a pseudonym, published nothing for twenty years, and then, at the age of seventy-seven, published *Good Behaviour* (under her own name), a rollicking good novel that was short-listed for the Man Booker Prize.

So, at what point, in these writers' long careers, might the farmer have pronounced them dog food? And what would he have done with Jean Rhys during her almost thirty years of silence between *Good Morning, Midnight* (1939) and *Wide Sargasso Sea* (1966)? Or with Doris Lessing when she veered off into Sufism and outer space?

The fact is, writers write (and publish) idiosyncratically. There are book-a-year writers, who might have one book in five one would want to reread, if any, and there are book-every-five-six-seven-year writers, who might hit it right with one of them. Or never. And so forth. Some writers persist into old age; others, many others, run out of strength, of heart, of heat. Even those strapped to the wheel by nature or by habit can find themselves—after years, decades—without the familiar leap in the blood, the joy, the lust, the demon hope.

"Now I am more conscious of the possibility that everything could be lost," said Alice Munro at the age of sixty-three, "that you could lose what had filled your life before ... It's something I never would have been able to think of losing twenty years ago—the faith, the desire ... It's not the giving up of the writing that I fear. It's the giving up of this excitement or whatever it is that ... makes you write."

What Munro seems to be talking about is not writer's block, but rather writer's fatigue, the dirty little secret whispered among older writers: I'm tired, I'm sick of it, not curious enough to go after something new the way I used to. Anyway, it's no longer, Who am I? I've found this out already. It's, Who are they? And do I care enough about them to find out, when what I really want is peace. To sit in a wicker chair looking out to sea. Or dig in the garden, unobliged to play spouse, parent, grandparent, host, or hostess, when all I want is to flee the things and the people that seem to hold me in place, to grab what's left of the life and make a run for it.

But where to? And won't I, without the work, feel life to be fraudulent? And, anyway, how will it be without work? Without even the pretense of work? The justification of it?

"I suppose," says Munro, "it's like when you don't fall in love anymore."

Perhaps. Or perhaps, like Troilus at the end of Chaucer's *Troilus and Criseyde*, the scope and scale of life has changed, the perception both of space and of time. There, in heaven, Troilus looks down with contemptus mundi at Criseyde running around with the Greeks, and at the little spot of earth on which he'd been slain. As he looks, he contemplates the vanity of the life left behind, the lust, the falsehood—everything that had mattered so much to him when he was alive.

Lust, or at least the erotic in its myriad forms, plays no small part in the life of the imagination. And so, when it begins to seep away, as inevitably it must, what is left to take its place? Ambition? Pride? Rage?

Rage would be my guess. Not the rage of regret, but the rage that comes with wasting time—squandering what's left of one's time on domestic chores, social obligations, or, worst of all, in working doggedly toward an inspiration that simply never arrives.

"I think it is a grave fault in life," wrote Philip Larkin, "that so much time is wasted in social matters, because it not only takes up time when you might be doing individual private things, but it prevents you storing up the psychic energy that can then be released to create art or whatever it is. It's terrible the way we scotch silence and solitude at every turn, quite suicidal. I can't see how to avoid it, without being very rich or very unpopular, and it does worry me, for time is slipping by, and nothing is done. It isn't as if anything was gained by this social frivolity. It isn't: it's just a waste."

"I've always found," said Rebecca West, "I've had too many family duties to enable me to write enough. I would have written much better and I would have written much more [without them]."

Contrary to what one may imagine, age, not youth, is more likely to be a time of scatter—of mind, of action, of intention, of desire, a version of what William James termed *zerrissenheit* (torn-to-pieces-hood). It used to be that one could field family, guests, phone calls, emails, never losing touch with the sort of deep, strong undercurrent that could always be counted on to carry one forward in one's work.

No longer. Now the impetus to work has to be terrified into life by a deadline. Or, failing that, by an attack of hope, the sort of hope that seems to come, if at all, with untrammeled time, free from the interruptions one seems, somehow and against all sense, to welcome in. As Seamus Deane put it to Nuala O'Faolain, "Endless charities with yourself as donation." But still, the question is, Why? Horror vacui? Horror of solitude? Of abandonment? Of loneliness and despair?

Just consider the sway exerted by adult children and their families over parents. Would this, could this have happened to those parents during the chain gang years of parenthood, when those children were young? Then, at least, a mother could be pitied for trying to snatch time back for herself. She was not expected to demonstrate a Troilus-like perspective at the sight of a grandchild throwing a tantrum or trying to twist the ear off a dog. Nor was she assumed to embrace with gladness the role of Quiet Old Bunny Knitting in a Rocking Chair and Whispering, "Hush."

It is a standard injunction in ancient Chinese classics of filial piety that adult children, when their parents are old and discontent, should crawl about on the floor, acting like children themselves in order to entertain the parents and make them feel young again.

I'm not sure that observing an adult child crawling around on the floor would achieve much for me. On the contrary, I recently found my arm rising through the air to give my forty-two-year-old daughter, behaving exceedingly childishly, a resounding slap across the cheek. Silence, at least for a few seconds. Blessed silence. After which, I was left wishing one could slap any number of people for any number of reasons.

But one can't, of course, at least not if one prefers to stay out of jail, or out of the hospital. One must simply content oneself with the sort of mutterings of complaint common to the agèd. Or behave like a child oneself, demanding, refusing, snatching away from others. Or just playing nicely with the toys one has at hand: pen, ink, paper, computer, dictionary, and, above all, words themselves.

The ability to play is essential to creativity. Why? How? Even Freud declared psychoanalysis unable to throw any light on the matter. What can be said is that creativity requires a sort of openness to discovery—a mood, a mode, a facility of mind free of preconception. By which I do not mean experimental writing, whatever that is. On this I am entirely of a mind with Anatole Broyard, who said, "When something is called experimental fiction, it generally means the experiment failed."

Words may be playthings—words and the thoughts to which they give form—but they are not to be taken lightly.

"You are surrounded by jargon," says V. S. Naipaul, "in the newspapers, in friends' conversations—and as a writer, you can become very lazy. You can start using words lazily."

"Expression," said Pope famously, "is the Dress of Thought," thus neatly representing the neoclassical position on poetic diction. Wordsworth, the Romantic, disagreed loudly. "If words be not . . . an incarnation of thought," he said, "but only a clothing for it, then surely will they prove an ill gift. Language, if it do not uphold, and feed, and leave in quiet, like the power of gravitation or the air we breathe, is a counter-spirit, unremittingly and noiselessly at work, to subvert, to lay waste, to vitiate, and to dissolve."

However words are considered, the facility to play with language, to keep it fresh, to keep it coming—this is the challenge to be faced as the years and the books accumulate. One of the dangers along the way lies in the fact that the words themselves can become old friends—too familiar, too taken for granted, too used to each other's company. And so they aren't such fun to play with any more. They refuse to surprise or to enchant.

The game lies in keeping language buoyant somehow. Those writers who continue writing well into old age—Beatrix Potter, P. D. James, Penelope Fitzgerald, Willa Cather, Saul Bellow, Philip Roth, V. S. Naipaul, John Updike, Gore Vidal, these just a few—those writers, whether or not the writing comes more slowly or as well, have found a way to stay alive *in* the writing, the demands of life notwithstanding.

"I have a certain amount of small-change intelligence which I carry around for the needs of the non-writing day," said Elizabeth Bowen. "But I am fully intelligent only when I write."

Others, like Whitman, Blake, and Montaigne spent much of their later years rearranging, rewriting, refashioning— essentially repeating—what they had written before. Yet others, like Truman Capote, managed to die before they had a chance to fade ("A good career move," said Gore Vidal, his nemesis.) And then there are those who simply stopped writing—or, at least, stopped writing fiction: Katherine Anne Porter after *Ship of Fools*, E. M. Forster after *A Passage to India* (whereafter, as it was said, his reputation went up with every book he didn't write.)

In the long-term stakes, however, those who come into full flower late—after five, ten, twenty books—are of a rarer species than are those who flare while young and then simply go on, book after book, into the distance.

Meanwhile, they are being watched, assessed, judged, and often found wanting by other writers. Here, for instance, is Henry James reviewing *Our Mutual Friend* in *The Nation*: "[This] is, to our perception, the poorest of Mr. Dickens's works. And it is poor with the poverty not of momentary embarrassment, but of permanent exhaustion. It is wanting in inspiration. For the last ten years it has seemed to us that Mr. Dickens has been unmistakably forcing himself. *Bleak House* was forced; *Little Dorrit* was labored; the present work is dug out as with a spade and pickaxe."

Which was written at a time when poets and novelists stood at the center of culture rather than on its periphery, before they had conceded the stage to Screenwriting, Slam Poetry, Performance Art, Rap, Video Games, and God knows what else.

And, predictably, James, in turn, came in for a deal of scorn himself. "Would you rather read Henry James," asked Lawrence Durrell, "or be crushed to death by a great weight?" "I am reading Henry James," said Virginia Woolf, " . . . and feel myself as one entombed in a block of smooth amber."

Woolf herself had much to say about old age. "Why yield a moment to regret or envy or worry?" she said, months before committing her body to the River Ouse. "Our old age is not going to be sunny orchard drowse . . . I detest the hardness of [it]—I feel it. I rasp. I'm tart . . . What I need is the old spurt."

"Always," writes Jack Gilbert in his wonderful poem "And She Waiting,"

Always I have been afraid
of this moment:
of the return to love
with perspective.

I see these breasts
with the others.
I touch this mouth
and the others.
I command this heart
as the others.
I know exactly
what to say.

Innocence has gone
out of me.
The song.
The song, suddenly,
has gone out
of me.

✱

AND YET, HERE is the song, this wonderfully minor-key lament. And there is something invigorating, too, in Woolf's

rasping tartness. The irascible, the disillusioned, the saga-
cious, the mordant, the meditative—in these can lie the
appeal in old age itself.

*

PERHAPS BECAUSE I grew up almost the youngest in a vast
family, I was accustomed to old age, comfortably familiar
with it, felt it moving with me through childhood and adolescence, at first like a benign shadow of the future ahead,
and then, as I grew older, as a sort of doppelganger. So that
I did not fear it as much as await its arrival with foresight,
bemusement, and, after a while, in anticipation of relief
from the exhaustion and frenzy of youth.

But then, in my mid-forties, I went to Crete, a place
whose history—half European, half African—had always
intrigued me. I went there alone, making a big deal of wanting ten days of solitude, no talk, at the other end of the
world. I went for a rest. And, not incidentally, to write a
travel essay.

On the night of my arrival, I made my way to the
hotel's charming alfresco restaurant, open on three sides to
the softness of the September evening. And stood there for
some minutes, waiting to be seated.

But the maître d' seemed deliberately not to be catching

my eye. After a while I began to feel like a teenage girl waiting to be asked to dance. And so I waved him over.

"Madame?"

The place was full of well-heeled European couples— men in signet rings and expensive loafers, their ample women bronzed and bejeweled. There were Germans, Swiss, French, some Italians. Except for the noise of a few raucous children, the talk was, on the whole, unanimated, desultory, conjugal. Clearly, this was the sort of place to which men brought their wives.

"A table for one, please," I said.

"Ah!" He hesitated for some seconds, and then headed off to a small table between the serving station and a bush. "Please," he said, pulling out a chair.

But I had not come halfway around the world to sit at a table behind a bush. Being chosen to dance is one thing; being chosen by the fat boy quite another. "No," I said. "I can see nothing from here."

Folkloric dancing was included in the so-called dining experience, and, even though I might have wished to sit this out behind that bush—not being at all keen on folkloric dancing, especially the sort that promises to include members of the audience, Zorba style—I would not, just because I was a woman alone, submit meekly to being placed out of sight.

I walked to an empty table that commanded not only the dance floor but also the sunset over the Mediterranean, the beach, a pod of Germans emerging from the water, a yacht anchored out in the bay. "Here," I said, sitting down. "I shall sit here."

It occurred to me, as the wine steward rolled into his spiel, that ten years ago this man might have found a way to sound me out, make suggestions on the sly. Now, he wouldn't dare. It had been a magical transformation, happening so gradually as to be hardly noticeable in the process. Like tooth decay. Still, there was real pleasure in the change. I could stroll into town without fielding flirtatious onslaughts from men. And I could sit now in solitary triumph at the premier table I had won for myself, order food and wine like a dowager. And I was content.

And then the pianist struck up "Hey, Jude" on a synthesizer, and suddenly I was alone in the middle of my life, thousands of miles from anyone to whom I mattered. Even the bored, prosperous couples all around me had at least old habits in common, old quarrels, their boredom itself.

Wine corks popped; cicadas sawed and screeched in the carob trees. The sunset had turned the whitewash of the hotel bungalows to a pinkish glow, and the air smelled of jasmine and lemon blossoms. The soup was excellent, the wine sharp and tannic. When the dancers arrived, stamping and yelping, I sat back in a sort of sad benignity of spirit. Tomorrow, I decided, I would start on the essay I had come to write. I would rent a car, drive around the island. And, although I had never been much of a tourist, glance through the guidebook after dinner, mark off what I thought I should see.

The car I rented was more like a motorized thimble. But it was thrilling to be off on my own, singing as I twisted and wound up mountain roads, stopping at a village here, a Byzantine church there, and then plunging downhill to a beach to have a swim. This, I decided—this freedom, this spontaneity, these days to myself—this was what I had come for. I had reached the plateau of my life—a few books behind me, a few more to come. And, with old age ambling amiably beside me, I had nothing to fear.

And then, on my last day, I decided to visit the Dictaean cave, purported birthplace of Zeus. There was a long, tortuous drive to get there, and then a hot, steep, slippery climb up to the entrance.

At the ticket booth, out of breath, I handed over my money. The ticket seller, a dapper middle-aged man with thick black moustaches, grasped my hand in his. "You Engrish?" he asked. "You need guide? Cave very dark and slipperish! Whoops!" He winked, gave my hand a squeeze. "You go alone, darling? You sure?"

I felt like Mrs. Stone enjoying the last day of her Roman Spring. But I didn't remove my hand; it seemed too ungrateful a gesture, too violent. Somehow, he had taken the money without loosening his grasp. I glanced at the line behind, hoping he'd give me my change, and release me. But he just lowered his voice.

"When you come out of cave, we have coffee, yes? You promise this for me?" With his left hand, he had handed me the ticket. "Four for the ticket," he murmured. "Okay?"

I nodded, and he let go. "Don't forget, darling!" he called after me. A sour-looking matron handed me a brown tallow candle for the cave. How many like me, I wondered, pass her every day? Women too craven, too embarrassed, to demand their change? I stopped for a moment, thinking I'd go back for it. But the line was moving. And, anyway, did I want another scene up there? For the equivalent of a dollar? Was my dignity worth that little?

And then, suddenly, there before me was the cave itself, a gigantic primordial chasm, not cave-like at all, not a slash in the side of a mountain, but an abyss hollowed deep down into its center, its yawning mouth and palate hoary with lichen and moss, and, farther in, giant bulging pillars of rock, black outcroppings, twists and turns. The air down there was stale, the ancient steps slick and steep. And, joining the procession of flickering candles snaking downward, I descended with the silent crowd, down into the chill, damp, terrifying darkness.

Considering that moment now, I am put in mind of a Levin cartoon I saw decades ago in *The New Yorker*. In it, the Grim Reaper, hooded, sickle in hand, has shown up at the door of an apartment. "Relax," he says to the woman in the doorway, "I've come for your toaster."

One might enjoy the same sort of reprieve, I suppose, if the *Paris Review* came calling, not to request an interview but to ask one to interview someone else. Whatever the case, and whether or not the writers had already done their best work when they were snagged, the interviews themselves can be wonderfully cheering, if only for the complaints and vituperations that abound within them—the loneliness, the sweat, the rage at critics, the jealousies, the disparagements, the disgruntled, resentful, envious rumpus of it all.

Only recently does it seem to have become fashionable to be gruntled with the writing life, to give voice to a sort of cheery good-will-all-round and admiration of the competition that seems more at home in Hollywood than in the world of letters. And, really, is there anything more boring? All those paeans to mentors? To the fellowship of other writers? Those joyful discoveries of truth on the page?

"Did you meet Yeats?" the interviewer asks Rebecca West.

"Yes," says she. "He wasn't a bit impressive and he wasn't any sort of person at all. He boomed at you like a foghorn."

"I find Faulkner intolerably bad," complains Evelyn Waugh. And, "I am reading Proust for the first time. Very poor stuff. I think he was mentally defective. I remember how small I used to feel when people talked about him and I didn't dare admit I couldn't get through him. Well, I can get through him now, of course—because I can read anything that isn't about politics. Well, the chap was plain barmy."

And then there is the despite for the aging self still at it, doggedly.

"After fifty," says Henry Green, "one ceases to digest; as someone once said: 'I just ferment my food now.' Most of us walk crabwise to meals and everything else. The oblique approach in middle age is the safest thing. The unusual at this period is to get anywhere at all—God damn!"

What about the exceptions, though? What about those writers who come suddenly, and without warning, into full power late in life? And how does this happen, this anomaly of the creative spirit? We don't know, we can't know the mystery that lies at the heart of creativity.

What we do know is that time runs out, and that worrying about it only engenders panic. Perhaps this is why there is so persistent a thrust toward turning the clock back: seventy the new sixty, sixty the new fifty, and so forth. Until, at about twenty, the equipoise seems to have been met, and childhood itself gallops forward to the same point: five the new ten, ten the new seventeen, etc.

So, where does this leave the writer in her sixth, seventh, eighth decade? Trying hard, in a life ever more beset by the din of large and small demands, to settle into the sort of silence that makes it possible to listen for her own voice? The sort of silence that, somehow, was so much more accessible in youth?

"Have you still got your space?" Doris Lessing asks new writers, "Your soul, your own and necessary place where your own voices may speak to you, you alone, where you may dream. Oh, hold on to it, don't let it go."

"I have three entire days alone," said Virginia Woolf, "three pure and rounded pearls . . . Three solitary nights. Think of that! Was there ever such a miracle? Not a voice, not a telephone. Only the owl calling; perhaps a clap of thunder, the horses going down to the Brooks, and Mr. Botten calling with the milk in the morning."

Acknowledgments

FOR THE GIFT OF TIME, PEACE, AND A BEAUTIFUL PLACE in which to write, I thank the Bogliasco Foundation, Civitella Ranieri, the Corporation of Yaddo, and the Spiti Logotexnias in Greece. Dan Smetanka has been a brick. And Claudia Ballard, with her enthusiasm and persistence, has seen me through. Thank you.

THANK YOU TO the following journals and publications for printing versions of these essays—sometimes in slightly different form:

"The Romance of Elsewhere," *Narrative*

"Keeping Watch," *Harper's Magazine*

"Useful Zulu Phrases, 1986," *Harper's Magazine*

"Gloria Mundi," *Ploughshares*

"Multiple Choice," *Living Fit*

"Letter from London," *Mirabella*

"Caveat Viator," *wowOwow*

"It's a Small, Unnatural World," *The New York Times*

"The Beach of the Lost World," *Allure*

"Honky, Napoleon, and the Empress Wu," *Harper's Magazine*

"Inheriting the Past," *House Beautiful*

"A Stranger in My House," *The New York Times Magazine*

"Viva Mandela!" *Elle*

"Running the Smalls Through," *The Other Woman* (Warner Books)

"Locked In," *The New York Times*

"Happy Birthday to Me," *Kiss Tomorrow Hello: Notes from the Midlife Underground* (Doubleday)

"Ignorance Chic," *Mirabella*

"Letter from Texas," *Mirabella*

"Doing No Harm: Some Thoughts on Reading and Writing in the Age of Umbrage," *Narrative*

"When Enough Is Enough: Age and the Creative Impulse," *Narrative*

About the Author

LYNN FREED has published seven novels, a collection of short fiction, and a collection of essays. Her work has appeared in *Harper's Magazine*, *The New Yorker*, and *The Atlantic*, among other publications. Her honors include the inaugural Katherine Anne Porter Award in fiction from the American Academy of Arts & Letters, two PEN/ O. Henry awards, and a Guggenheim Foundation fellowship. Born in South Africa, she now lives in Northern California.

Printed in the United States
by Baker & Taylor Publisher Services